MW01485805

Community
CONSCIOUS
Policing

THE GREAT BOOK OF DIVINE ORDINANCES
THE CODE OF HUMAN BEHAVIOR
TRANSLATION OF THE PAPYRI NW, NBSNI, AND INSA

1. Thou shall not cause suffering to humans
2. Thou shall not cause intrigue by ambition
3. Thou shall not deprive a poor person of their subsistence
4. Thou shall not commit acts that are loathed by the Gods
5. Thou shall not cause suffering to others
6. Thou shall not steal offerings from temples
7. Thou shall not steal bread meant for Gods
8. Thou shall not steal offerings destined to sanctify spirits
9. Thou shall not commit shameful acts inside the sacro-saints of temples
10. Thou shall not sin against nature with one's own kind
11. Thou shall not take milk from the mouth of a child
12. Thou shall not fish using other fish as bait
13. Thou shall not extinguish fire when it should burn
14. Thou shall not violate the rules of meat offerings
15. Thou shall not take possession of properties belonging to temples and Gods
16. Thou shall not prevent a God from manifesting itself
17. Thou shall not cause crying
18. Thou shall not make scornful signs
19. Thou shall not get angry or enter a dispute without just cause
20. Thou shall not be impure
21. Thou shall not refuse to listen to the words of justice and truth
22. Thou shall not blaspheme
23. Thou shall not sin by excess speech
24. Thou shall not speak scornfully
25. Thou shall not curse a Divinity
26. Thou shall not cheat on the offerings to the Gods
27. Thou shall not waste the offerings to the dead
28. Thou shall not snatch food from children and thou shall not sin against the Gods of one's city
29. Thou shall not kill Divine animals with bad intentions
30. Thou shall not cheat
31. Thou shall not rob or loot
32. Thou shall not steal
33. Thou shall not kill
34. Thou shall not destroy offerings
35. Thou shall not reduce measurements
36. Thou shall not steal properties belonging to Gods
37. Thou shall not lie
38. Thou shall not snatch food away or wealth
39. Thou shall not cause pain
40. Thou shall not fornicate with the fornicator
41. Thou shall not act dishonestly
42. Thou shall not transgress
43. Thou shall not act maliciously
44. Thou shall not steal farmlands
45. Thou shall not reveal secrets
46. Thou shall not court a man's wife
47. Thou shall not sleep with another's wife
48. Thou shall not cause terror
49. Thou shall not rebel
50. Thou shall not be the cause of anger or hot tempers
51. Thou shall not act with insolence
52. Thou shall not cause misunderstandings
53. Thou shall not misjudge or judge hastily
54. Thou shall not be impatient
55. Thou shall not cause illness or wounds
56. Thou shall not curse a king
57. Thou shall not cloud drinking water
58. Thou shall not dispossess
59. Thou shall not use violence against family
60. Thou shall not frequent wickeds
61. Thou shall not substitute injustice for justice
62. Thou shall not commit crimes
63. Thou shall not overwork others for one's gain
64. Thou shall not mistreat their servants
65. Thou shall not menace
66. Thou shall not allow a servant to be mistreated by his master
67. Thou shall not induce famine
68. Thou shall not get angry
69. Thou shall not kill or order a murder
70. Thou shall not commit abominable acts
71. Thou shall not commit treason
72. Thou shall not try to increase one's domain by using illegal means
73. Thou shall not usurp funds and property of others
74. Thou shall not seize on cattle on the prairies
75. Thou shall not trap poultry that are destined to Gods
76. Thou shall not obstruct water in the moment it is supposed to run
77. Thou shall not break dams that are established on current waters

Community
CONSCIOUS
Policing

A GUIDE FOR PEOPLE'S JUSTICE
AND LAW ENFORCEMENT SOLUTIONS

By

BRANDON LEE 32°, M.A.T.

Training 4 Transformation, LLC

www.T4TSavesLives.com

Community Conscious Policing™

Community Conscious Policing is a public health–centered response model intended to end unnecessary and inappropriate law enforcement violence.

It is designed to augment and enhance existing continuing education for law enforcement, students in social justice–related fields, advocates involved in police accountability, and organizations seeking to increase their outreach capacity.

Our innovative training curriculum is designed with the input of sworn police trainers and thousands of diverse community participants whom we brought together during very polarizing times to design a new training process based on experiential learning.

This model is a culturally responsive, trauma-healing approach to community and civic engagement based on the founders' conscious leadership principles. These include emotional intelligence, experiential learning, decolonizing strategies, and mindfulness practices that transcend traditional barriers.

T4T is a community-led organization that trains law enforcement alongside the people they serve. We center the lived experience of diverse communities who have historically been most impacted by law enforcement and the criminal justice system.

Copyright © 2021 Brandon Lee

All rights reserved. No part of this publication may be reproduced, distributed, or transmitted in any form or by any means, including photocopying, recording, or other electronic or mechanical methods, without the prior written permission of the publisher, except in the case of brief quotations embodied in critical reviews and certain other noncommercial uses permitted by copyright law. For permission requests, write to the publisher, addressed "Attention: Permissions Coordinator," at the web or email address below.

www.T4TSavesLives.com

ISBN: 978-0-578-94069-4 (print)
ISBN: 978-0-578-94218-6 (ebook)

Ordering Information:
Special discounts are available on quantity purchases by corporations, associations, schools and others.
For details, contact Info@Train4Transformation.com or www.T4TSavesLives.com.

Dedication

It takes a village to raise a child."—Proverb

This book is dedicated to my loving wife and children. Thank you for believing in Papa. My world begins and ends with you!

To my mentors, both professional and personal, your efforts, time, wisdom, and invaluable guidance are truly appreciated. Thank you Resmaa Menakem, author of *My Grandmother's Hands*, for helping Black men articulate how to heal from the trauma of racism. Thank you Iyanla Vanzant, thought leader and spiritual teacher from TV show Fix My Life, for demonstrating the power of trauma-healing combined with experiential learning and traditional wisdom. To activists, poets and artists like Climbing Poetree, Sunni Patterson and Anida Yoeu Ali, your passion and liberation are contagious. Thank you for the inspiration to liberate ourselves and chase our dreams!

Most especially, I would like to honor the ancestors, who thoroughly prepared us for this game called life. Rize in Power to our sister and comrade in social justice, Angela Berkfield. To Aunt Johnie Mae and Uncle "Little Brother" Cook who stepped up for me after my dad passed away, your sacrifice is truly appreciated.

This book is dedicated in the loving memory of my father James William Lee Jr., grandmother Wilmerteen Cook, grandfather Jimmy E. Rowe Sr., and grandmother Betty Rowe. We honor the Ancestors for standing up in the face of adversity so we could sit down.

It's our turn now....

Table of Contents

Introduction

The polarization of law enforcement and community members deepens as the nation continues to erupt into protests and uprisings. Trust has been broken and communities feel unsafe. It is easy to identify the problem. The real question is, "What is the solution?" <u>Community Conscious Policing</u> is a public health–centered response model intended to end unnecessary and inappropriate law enforcement violence.

Through this model, participants work together toward a shared vision of community by confronting their own biases, dismantling outdated systems and narratives, and engaging in honest discussions without the power dynamics associated with uniforms and guns. This shared vision could be led by community members who understand the dynamics and stakeholders involved.

This is not work that can simply be learned with a college degree. One has to plug into the generations of elders who walked this path before us. Being from Oakland and being a member of historically Black organizations most certainly prepared Brandon for this journey from police accountability to law enforcement training.

Diversity training based on implicit bias and intellectual doctrines do not include members of the community. Officers are never exposed in a training context to people who have different identities than themselves. They therefore cannot begin to develop empathy for the people they are supposed to serve.

Officers rarely sit in a room with diverse community members they serve without an unequal power dynamic, which condones the use of lethal force without accountability. Current police training on diversity generally serves to shield law enforcement officers and agencies from accountability and prosecution. These are problems to watch for when evaluating the quality of police accountability efforts. For every effort toward accountability and justice made, there is another manifestation of prejudice, institutional racism, or inequality.

What distinguishes Community Conscious Policing from other models is that it works in both police accountability and training. It incorporates lessons learned from diverse community perspectives into law enforcement training, which can then be enforced through policy.

Facilitators must be diverse community members who have track records of removing barriers and creating access for affected people. Trainers are encouraged to share their testimony directly with decision makers in local law enforcement through the experiential learning exercises. In exchange, community members learn more about the challenges facing police and are given tips on how to better engage with them.

The Importance of Initiation

Without initiation, this work is not possible. The intersectionality of police accountability reform and trauma healing work is indigenous initiatic wisdom. It is the White male dominated modern paradigm that generated the state sponsored barbarism that is police brutality. Solutions to the police killings will not come from the same place.

It is necessary to reconnect with the life-giving philosophies that uncolonized indigenous people have preserved in ancient living tradition. It is only these life-giving philosophies, found in the initiation camps, that will generate life preserving solutions for our modern problem of police brutality.

One cannot clean poop off of their body with urine. One must use pure clean water. Similarly the modern paradigm will not hold the solutions. Humbly look to the Ancestors and the elders for the philosophies that preserve life, to move forward. The difference between Community Conscious Policing and others is that our policies, procedures, and practices were given birth through the initiation of its founders in deep old world wisdom: pre-imperialist, pre-colonial, and pre-Greco Roman philosophy.

This is why civilian oversight review boards are not a one size fits all solution offered to communities; it is just one of an endless supply of tactics used to apply life preserving principles to the evils facing humanity, in this case, police brutality.

The two pillars of the work are to eliminate violence and to restore genuine trust between the best of law enforcement and the communities who are most impacted by them, not just a reduction in taxpayer liabilities. It is necessary to address the culture of violence that creates the conditions under which police brutality against oppressed peoples becomes acceptable.

Brandon Lee has spent most of his life and energy fighting law enforcement on racial profiling cases. He knows it is his calling to be proactive in saving lives and reducing violence and trauma. He teaches people to have self-worth, to be observant of their own physical state, and to honor their own intuition when they experience bias, racism, and injustice in order not to succumb to the pressures associated with seeking police accountability.

Brandon was the first Grand Historian appointed to the M.W. Prince Hall Grand Lodge of Free and Accepted Masons (F&AM) for the states of Oregon, Idaho, and Montana Jurisdiction. His office involved the archiving of documents and artifacts, and the publishing of historical information related to the order. "There is a direct correlation between the growth of the number of successful African Americans, and the development of Prince Hall Freemasonry (Hairston 2013)."

Prior to affiliating in Portland, Brandon was raised a Prince Hall Freemason in Texas. According to Alonza Tehuti Evans, past Grand Historian and Archivist of the Most Worshipful Prince Hall Grand Lodge of the District of Columbia and co-author of *The History of the Most Worshipful Prince Hall Grand Lodge, District of Columbia, 1823-2014*, "The Order of Prince Hall Freemasonry is the oldest recognized and continuously active organization founded by Africans in America. As early as 1784, it laid the foundation for black citizenship, education, and the improvement of the social and economic conditions of the black community" (Library of Congress, 2017).

At Harvard Square in Cambridge Common in Massachusetts, there is a monument erected to Prince Hall and dedicated to thousands of Black revolutionary patriots who helped lay the foundation of this country. Prince Hall, considered the founder of Black Freemasonry, was born circa 1735, and upon winning his freedom petitioned to join Washington's Army. Later, he founded the first Black elementary school in Cambridge, Massachusetts. Prince Hall's contributions were such that the Cambridge City Council posthumously declared Prince Hall to be one of the United States of America's Founding Fathers.

Brandon discovered the Order of Prince Hall Freemasonry after pledging his collegiate fraternity, Kappa Alpha Psi Fraternity, Inc. In 1911, a group of Black students who attended Indiana University founded this historically Black fraternity, which is humbly referred to by its members as "the bond," to defend themselves from extreme acts of prejudice and discrimination. Back then, the vigilante lynching of Black people was commonplace and Indiana was saturated in racism (Kappa Alpha Psi Fraternity, 2021). Through his initiations, Brandon discovered a path of decolonization and liberation that is the foundation of Community Conscious Policing.

Apply Life-Giving Principles: Ban Deadly Force

There is one notion that is not taught in any modern university or book: the human mind is incapable of creation; it can only imitate. This is according to Kemetic (the Pharaonic culture of the Nile and Niger Valleys) Temples. This runs directly counter to the egoism taught and sold throughout all levels of modern society. Human minds only reorganize what they have been exposed to. New things result from mistakes in the copying process, but this can hardly be called creation or invention.

For this reason, to find solutions, one needs to go outside of the problem's modern paradigm. Indigenous cultures that were oriented towards living in harmony with the earth and preserving life can provide a model to follow while working to stop police killings.

The Kemetic philosophy and perspective present comes from Neb Naba Lamoussa Morodenibig, an authentic and exceptionally gifted Dogon High

Priest, who founded the Earth Center in 1996. The Earth Center is a non-profit organization headquartered in Ouagadougou, Burkina Faso, authorized by His Majesty Yoabili, the 34th King of the Gulmu throne. It exists to bring the ancestral and initiatic knowledge out from the secrecy of the African bush, and reintroduce humanity's original culture, Kemetic culture, to the world. The Earth Center has branches in West Africa, the U.S., Canada, and the United Kingdom (The Earth Center, 1999).

This is a message for America, Europe, and the modern world from the Bobo-Dioulasso Royal Court, delivered to the Earth Center Delegation during the 2012 Spiritual Pilgrimage to Burkina Faso. It was relayed by Nehez Meniooh, Director of the Earth Center's MTAM School of Mystery:

> "Tell them the ancestors are alive in us and our ancestors are in harmony. We come from the same place. That's why you're able to sit here now. You see us here [and] now. We have harmony. We're not fighting.
>
> Whatever they were telling you, like we were the ones to send you out [to enslavement], don't listen to that because if that's true we couldn't have this harmony now. We've been waiting for you guys to come home.
>
> Bring our message to everybody out there. Let them know that the way we live is a choice. The way we live is not because we are short-handed. It's not because we lack resources. It's not because we wish we were in the shoes of the people in the colonial world.
>
> We choose to live this way, to live simply, to live humbly, because we are the ones connected to nature like this. We're the ones holding what our ancestors gave us like this. We wouldn't trade this for anything. Make sure everybody knows we are not suffering like this, this is what we choose to do.
>
> Make sure they all know, we haven't lost anything. If they're interested in finding themselves, we're here to receive them because we haven't lost anything."

This is the Kemetic renaissance taking place right now. That's why the Earth Center is here. There are over 100 books written about the Dogon, but they are written by outsiders, researchers, and academics with their own agendas. The exceptions were written by Naba, a Gourmantche from Fada N'Gourma, Burkina Faso, West Africa. The Naba bloodline is very old and is mentioned in high regard as Nebaioth (Nabatean) in the King James version of the Bible, Book of Isaiah, chapter 60, verse 7, "All the flocks of Kedar shall be gathered together unto thee, the rams of Nebaioth shall minister unto thee: they shall come up with acceptance on mine altar, and I will glorify the house of my glory" (Bible Hub). The Gourmantche are a subset of the larger Dagomba (Dogon) people.

Naba is the only member of the Dogon bloodlines to write books about his own culture. The Naba bloodline in particular is revered because of their skill and discipline in astronomy, geomancy, parapsychology, metaphysics, and timekeeping. This made them suitable to manage the spiritual affairs of the Pharaoh. To this day, the Naba bloodline is respected by royalty for how pure they kept the teachings and well they maintained their spiritual obligations.

At the core of Kemetic culture one finds the 77 Commandments. Kemetic people follow these Divine Ordinances, and it's culture that prioritizes the preservation of life over all other things. Modern Western culture, by contrast, values financial capital over life and nature.

Modern laws that govern policing authorize the use of deadly force to prevent escape, affect an arrest, defend against threat, etc. From the Kemetic perspective, the use of deadly force isn't authorized. In The Great Book of Divine Ordinances: The Code of Human Behavior, republished in 1999 by Prophet Naba, Commandment 33, "Thou shall not kill," and Commandment 69, "Thou shall not kill or order a murder," prohibit the use of deadly force for everyone from the common person to the king of kings. No one is exempt.

Applying principles that value preservation of life above all else tells one that they should prohibit the use of deadly force in policing without exceptions. The new vision of the world is one in which one group of people does not use deadly force to police another group of people, and the preservation of life is valued over all other financial concerns.

The 13th Amendment of the U.S. Constitution, however, authorizes slavery and involuntary servitude "as a punishment for crime" (National Constitution Center). This amendment makes it acceptable to use involuntary servitude, which is the use or threat of physical restraint, physical injury, coercion through law or the legal process for individuals convicted of crimes. It authorizes the use of forms of compulsory labor similar to African American slavery on people labeled criminals.

This is wrong and goes against the preservation of life. Police killings and the civil unrest they create are the only inevitable outcome of laws that authorize threats, restraints, injuries, and coercion. Let's not wait and make our children fix this problem.

Applying Commandments 1, "Thou shall not cause suffering to humans"; 55, "Thou shall not cause illness or wounds"; 63, "Thou shall not overwork others for one's gain"; and 66, "Thou shall not allow a servant to be mistreated by his master," the 13th Amendment should state: Neither slavery nor involuntary servitude shall exist within the United States, or any place subject to its jurisdiction.

Making this change would sever the roots of police brutality and the legal basis justifying police killings. Constantly apply principles that value the preservation of life above all else.

Chapter 1

Objectives for the Reader

The subject of this book is Community Conscious Policing, its origins, the experiences of founder Brandon Lee, and the Community Conscious Policing training model, which the reader can integrate into their actions to fight injustice and inequality.

We have included ways to engage in authentic and meaningful exchanges that will build rapport and increase understanding. The recounted experiences will show you how to identify and challenge stereotypes, assumptions, and prejudices regarding specific community groups and police officers.

Efforts to humanize the experiences of both community members and law enforcement officers have been made throughout the text. This story will help you identify concrete solutions such as policy changes, legislation, hiring practices, budget allocation, and community engagement that will further relationship building between law enforcement and the communities they serve. The goal is to provide the reader with the tools to make a personal commitment toward building a shared vision of community.

There is often conflict between law enforcement, community groups, and survivors of police brutality. The conflict is worsening as tensions between communities and police departments increase due to videos of police brutality going viral on social media.

In the midst of public outcry, Brandon has been able to deliver community-led police accountability training to a larger number of participants, bringing opposing sides together in meaningful dialogue that produces action.

The ideas expressed in this book are practical. They are derived and tempered from the author's lived experiences as a survivor of police brutality. Brandon Lee has education and professional experience in community organizing, public policy, business, international training, ethics, mediation, and redress.

The Problem of the Day

Eight thousand, seven hundred, and sixty-five people were killed by the police in the U.S. from January 1, 2013, to December 31, 2020, according to Mapping Police Violence a website that sourced its information from FatalEncounters.org, the U.S. Police Shootings Database, and KilledbyPolice.net, the three largest impartial crowdsourced databases of police killings. This should constitute some kind of state sponsored mass murder, war crime, or crime against humanity. That's not all.

In May 2021, for the same period of time UnidosUS, a Latino civil rights and advocacy organization, in partnership with the Raza Database Project, a network of 50 researchers, scholars, journalists, activists, and family members of victims killed by police, found that 16,273 people were killed by police. This is twice the previous number, and begs the question why and how can law enforcement be stopped from covering up police killings.

In the U.S., one is innocent until proven guilty in a court of law, so those killed by police were innocent. Most of the dead were killed in an arrest gone wrong. Only 75 of them were charged with crimes that weren't acquitted, reports MappingPoliceViolence.org. Over 99 percent were innocent deaths.

According to "The Counted," *The Guardian*'s tally of U.S. police killings, 1,146 people in the United States were killed by police in 2015. Three hundred and seven were Black, 584 White, 195 Hispanic/Latino, 13 Native Americans, 28 Asian/Pacific Islander, and 18 Other/Unknown (*The Guardian*, 2015). If you're Black, you're three times as likely to be killed by a cop than a White person (Harvard, 2020), but there are more Whites killed each year (Police Violence Report, 2020).

"The Counted" also reports 1,093 people in the U.S. were killed by police in 2016. Twenty-four were Native American, 266 were Black, 183 were Hispanic/Latino, 574 were White, 24 were Asian/Pacific Islander, and 22 were Other/Unknown (*The Guardian,* 2016). It seems that no demographic is safe when it comes to the issue of police killings. This is something everyone has a vested interest in because anyone can be killed by the police.

This equates to an average of three to six people killed every day by law enforcement officers in the United States, and even more are brutalized. Some officers are serving as judge, jury, and executioner. This should not be tolerated. Together, these acts constitute *police terrorism.*

Merriam-Webster dictionary defines "terror" as "a state of intense or overwhelming fear" and "violence or the threat of violence used as a weapon of intimidation or coercion." Police in the United States systematically use these tactics on unarmed people daily.

Humanity has dealt with the problem of terror for a long time. The Kemetic text The Great Book of Divine Ordinances: The Code of Human Behavior, the archetype of books and laws, is a text more than 150,000 years old. It was republished by the Earth Center 1999. It states this rule to govern humanity: "48. Thou shall not cause terror." Since Pharaonic times, humanity has been dealing with this issue. From then until now humanity hasn't progressed.

Cambyses II, a Persian conqueror, invaded the Nile Valley in 400 BC and set up laws to force Blacks to obey him as their new Pharaoh. He ordered his army to block entry to the temples for worship and commanded that any person who entered be killed.

This is the first occurrence recorded by the Kemetic temples of a person imposing and enforcing laws through the threat of death. There is a notion in Kemetic spirituality of the "becoming of existence" governed by the God Khepra. The principle of becoming states that there is no end to an action. Every action has consequences and effects that continue to affect everything in existence throughout time. As a result, even the smallest of human actions has the possibility to create great harm, either purposefully or inadvertently.

Cambyses was the first to enforce laws with death and in doing so he created the model followed globally by leaders and law enforcement throughout history until today: issue laws and make the population obey them with force. For this reason, Cambyses is considered by Kemetic philosophy the most evil person in history, with his actions still resulting in the deaths of so many. Cambyses' actions are still being replicated today as police killings.

In *Philosophy Podium*, Naba states, "If you were presented with two people, one considered a criminal (because he had killed innocent people) and the other considered a hero (because he had killed the criminal), your subconscious would no longer consider killing to be a crime" (Philosophy Podium, 2008). In modern society, the cop is considered the hero and the Black man is the criminal, leading to the police killings seen now. This subconscious decriminalization of killing has allowed leaders to create a system that kills innocent people (people who have not been charged or convicted), without accountability.

For this reason, a society of laws is not viable. A society that enforces laws and protects property by killing will fail. To have a viable society, all members must commit to preserving life over all other concerns. So, the author asks that every law enforcement officer and every individual commit to preserving life as their first priority in all circumstances.

Sir Robert Peel's Policing Principles

In 1829 the world's first modern police force was established in London by the Metropolitan Police Act of 1829 introduced by Sir Robert Peel. From this law, Sir Robert Peel's Nine Principles of Policing were derived (CLEJ, 2004). Upon close examination of these principles, juxtaposing them with the backdrop of daily police killings in the U.S., it can be concluded that U.S. Law Enforcement has failed to live up to Robert Peel's Principles.

For example, police are supposed to be an alternative to suppression of crime and disorder by the military and severe legal punishment. However, U.S. police venerate and follow the military, adopting their training and buying their weapons. Is there any wonder that death is the result? Now U.S. police are adding robots to their list of equipment they can use to hurt people – it's despicable.

U.S. police have forgotten that they depend on the public's approval of their existence, actions, behavior, and on their ability to maintain the public's respect, not on the number of arrests. Therefore, police shouldn't be incentivized to make arrests with raises, rank, and benefits. Police should be incentivized to maintain low crime rates without drawing a firearm or using force.

When U.S. police fail to obtain the respect of the community they brutalize, they lose the willing cooperation of that community. This inevitably leads to an escalation of the use of force, which loses the respect and cooperation of the public further, and a deadly cycle ensues.

Police are supposed to use the minimal amount of force in their duties.

When police unions usurp the powers of the judiciary to punish officers, those unions violate Robert Peel's Policing Principles. Not only do they lose the public's respect, and therefore the ability to police effectively, they corrupt the functions of government to the extent that the public loses faith in the judiciary and legislature as well.

U.S. law enforcement has forgotten that "the test of police efficiency is the absence of crime and disorder, and not the visible evidence of police action in dealing with them," reads Robert Peel's ninth principle as it appears on the Law Enforcement Action Partnership website. High arrest numbers, large police budgets, large police departments, and increased use of military weapons and equipment are evidence that U.S. law enforcement has failed.

There is one major problem with Sir Robert Peel's fifth principle, which states police should enforce the law "without regard to the justice or injustice of the substance of individual laws."

Referring to the principle of preserving life, Commandment 61 states, "Thou shall not substitute injustice for justice." Robert Peel's principle egregiously violates this Commandment. Legislatures should not make unjust laws and lawmakers should be held accountable for doing so. Police should not enforce unjust laws and should also be held accountable for doing so. It was this notion present in the birth of modern policing, the enforcement of unjust laws, that turned police into unjust killers in modern societies. It's time to fix this.

A History of U.S. Policing

A pattern of brutality and lethal violence against Black people in the U.S. can be traced back to slavery and the discriminatory "Black Codes" legislation, that followed (Hassett-Walker, 2019). Law enforcement institutions were modeled on the policies, procedures, and practices of slave patrols. This happened after the Emancipation Proclamation to regenerate the oppressive institutions of Confederate slavery in a new political climate that didn't tolerate overt slavery.

Slave patrols became police patrols—it was the same activity under a different name. After 200,000 freed men (Black ex-enslaved people) joined the Union Army during the Civil War (National Archives, 1999) and did what the U.S. government could not do—deliver a decisive victory against the Confederate South—General William Tecumseh Sherman issued Special Order No. 15, dated January 16, 1865. This order was reparations to freed Blacks. President Andrew Johnson revoked this order (New Georgia Encyclopedia).

Johnson redistributed reparations to the Confederate Aristocracy, ex–slave owners, ex–Confederate officials, war criminals, traitors, murderers, and those guilty of cruel and unusual punishment. These individuals would have faced execution for their crimes. Johnson did this by issuing his May 29, 1865, "Proclamation of Pardon and Amnesty" and subsequent proclamations. The details of these pardons were presented in 1998 by Dr. Kathleen Rosa Zebley in her dissertation "Rebel Salvation: The Story of Confederate Pardons" (Zebley, 1998). Johnson's intention was to pardon all the ex–slave owners and high-ranking ex-Confederates. The enforcement of these 13,500 issued pardons and 200,000 oaths of amnesty constituted the birth of industrialized police brutality and maintained economic injustice against Black people.

On January 22, 1883 the U.S. Supreme Court failed to uphold the Force Act designed to protect Black people against violent terrorism. The Court instead dismissed charges of murder and assault among others against a Tennessee Sheriff and his co-conspirators in the case United States v. Harris. This made the Court complicit in these acts of police terror and is an example of the systemic racism pervasive in the judicial branch of government.

The following story comes from the Tulsa Historical Society and Museums about the 1921 Tulsa Race Massacre, also known as the Tulsa Race Riot, in Tulsa, Oklahoma. This is commonly referred to as the "Bombing of Black Wall Street." There is no part of this massacre where law enforcement isn't involved in biased policing, racism, oppression, police brutality, police killing, and police cover-up.

On May 30, 1921, Dick Rowland, a Black man, rode the elevator of the Drexel Building with a White woman Sarah Page. After rumors spread, police arrested Dick the following day on erroneous charges, which were later dismissed. Inflammatory reporting in the May 31 *Tulsa Tribune* led to confrontations between armed groups of Blacks and Whites while the sheriff and his men barricaded the top floor to protect Rowland.

Shots were fired, and the outnumbered Blacks fled home to Greenwood. Municipal and county authorities failed to act and stop the violence. Civil officials deputized Whites only as law enforcement officers, some of them rioters, to participate in the violence while public officials provided Whites only with firearms and ammunition.

For 24 hours, White rioters burned and looted Greenwood on June 1, 1921. Governor Robertson implemented martial law, and had National Guardsmen imprison the 6,000 Black residents of Greenwood for eight days while looters and government agents stole everything. Thirty-five city blocks were burned to ruin, more than 800 people were treated for injuries from the assault, and an estimated 300 people were killed. One thousand two hundred fifty-six homes were burned by rioters and agents of the government in addition to all of the adjacent buildings composing that community.

The following is from *The Tulsa Race Riot and Three of Its Victims* by B.C. Franklin, a manuscript held at the Smithsonian Institute:

"I could see planes circling in mid-air. They grew in number and hummed, darted and dipped low. I could hear something like hail falling upon the top of my office building. Down East Archer, I saw the old Mid-Way hotel on fire, burning from its top, and then another and another and another building began to burn from their top."

15

From 1956–1971, the FBI's Counterintelligence Program, COINTEL-PRO, attempted to control Black people in the U.S. by assassinating or otherwise neutralizing Black leaders via false criminal charges and public humiliation. Redacted COINTELPRO files can be readily accessed on the FBI's website.

In 1985 the Philadelphia Police Department dropped military grade explosives on the MOVE organization in a West Philadelphia residential neighborhood. After the bomb dropped, the police chief and first responders let the fire burn purposefully.

The bomb and subsequent fires killed 11 people and destroyed more than 60 adjacent homes. The families affected were innocent people who were not involved. The homes and lives of the destroyed neighborhood weren't worth protecting in the eyes of decision-makers. Bryan Bentley wrote about this in his 2014 thesis, "Old Attitudes and New Beginnings: The Philadelphia Police and M O V E: 1972-1992."

In this act, police in the U.S. proved that they will kill and burn the homes of innocent people throughout a neighborhood to make an arrest.

The 1980s and '90s in Oakland, California, were commonly referred to as the dope era. The crack epidemic, the rise of HIV and AIDS, the 1994 crime bill, and the "three strikes" law led to the mass incarceration of Black and Brown people. It wreaked havoc on Black and Brown communities (Brennan Center for Justice, 2018).

The Department of Justice's Office of Community Oriented Policing Services has invested $14 billion into local police departments' efforts to improve community relations. Despite this influx of funds, the public's confidence in law enforcement has reached an all time low since the office's founding in 1993. According to Tony Cheng in *Input without Influence: The Silence and Scripts of Police and Community Relations.* "Eight years later, however, there is no sign of meaningful change, at least on the national level. The number of police killings has hovered around 1,100 every year since 2013, according to Mapping Police Violence, a research and advocacy group." (A Washington Post database shows a similar pattern.)

On May 6, 2012, Oakland police officer Miguel Masso—who resigned from the NYPD after settling a lawsuit for repeatedly beating and tasing Rafael Santiago—shot and killed 18-year-old African American high school student Alan Blueford in East Oakland. Masso then shot himself in the foot to cover up the killing (Oakland Wiki).

In 2015, Louisiana Officer Derek Stafford received an unprecedented 40-year prison sentence for killing Jeremy Mardis, a six-year-old boy (Stole, 2017).

On December 7, 2015, Oakland Police conspired to cover up an illegal home invasion by drunk cops Cullen Faeth and another unidentified officer who terrorized Olga and Nemesio Cortez (abc7, 2016).

In Harvey County, Oregon, in June 2016, disgraced Police Chief Larry O'Dea retired after being the subject of criminal investigations for shooting his friend while off-duty and for neglecting to report racist comments made by the Harney County Police Bureau's diversity manager (Associated Press, 2016).

According to a *Los Angeles Times* analysis of the California Department of Justice statistics, California law enforcement rejected nearly every racial-profiling complaint received from 2016–2019 (Los Angeles Times, 2020). It is important to highlight and uplift scenarios of biased police that don't necessarily result in brutality because they are linked to practices of systemic injustice.

In 2017, Oklahoma troopers assaulted a deaf man, Pearl Pearson, Jr., when he failed to comply with verbal instructions (Franklin 2018).

On March 16, 2017, Rodney Hess streamed his own death video on Facebook Live, when he was fatally shot by Crockett County Sheriff's Department (Ellis, 2017).

On March 27, 2017, three hours after Florida Police Officers told Latina Herring to stop repeatedly calling 911 for help, she and her four-year-old son were fatally shot by her boyfriend, Allen Cashe (Hadley, 2017).

On April 12, 2017, New York State Court of Appeals Associate Justice Sheila Abdus-Salaam, the first Black woman elected to New York State's highest court, who had a history of holding cops accountable, was found dead in the Hudson River. Her death was later ruled a suicide (Feuer, 2017).

In 2020, during the global pandemic of COVID-19, the nation saw community uprisings against police brutality and even local government entities voting to abolish or defund law enforcement (Gottbrath, 2020).

It is only in more recent years, through grassroots efforts and the courageous actions of reporters, activists, and lawyers, that it is now possible to get a picture of police brutality against Black people. Unfortunately, the problem does not stop there.

Some data on police brutality against Black people has been made public, but there is no data on how many Black trans women, Native women, Latinx communities, and people experiencing mental health crises have been brutalized and murdered by law enforcement officers. There is very little information available.

That makes this work urgent.

Clear, researched, and verifiable data regarding how many people are killed and brutalized by the police is hard to come by: law enforcement agencies redact, classify, and implement institutional measures to obscure the statistics so the public remains uninformed. Officers are protected from the repercussions of misconduct by police unions that lobby for them, giving them license to repeatedly brutalize with no recourse. In many cases, there are laws written to protect the police, hide their identities, hide or destroy their personnel files, and shield them from prosecution (*USA Today*, 2020).

The cycles of violence will continue until decision-makers begin shifting their approach to problem solving and fund community programs led by people who are closest to the pain. These populations bring lived, educational, and professional experience to inform law enforcement on what works best in Black and Brown neighborhoods. Those who survived homicides, drugs, racism in public health, and police brutality had to learn how to navigate law enforcement systems.

Many people see police as a force that protects them. My question is, "Are you willing to learn something new?" If the answer is "yes," then please continue reading because there's probably a huge unaddressed problem. This issue is outlined in detail and there are more than 100 references at the end of this book. Please check them as well.

The insights and experiences gained through the years are contained within the following pages. Through these stories, you can strengthen your efforts to bring accountability to the police in your community.

Chapter 2

Why Should White People Care?

First the term White must be defined. According to the Kemetic Temples, until 75 B.C., people on Earth were not classified in terms of color. Roman conquerors, after studying the spirituality of temples in the Nile Valley, found that the color white was considered a symbol of the absence of color. It symbolizes purity and is associated with innocence.

Romans, who had no hygiene practices, paper, or written language before they were taught by the Kemetic priesthood and Pharaonic culture, claimed whiteness in an attempt to prove Roman worth, while failing to conquer pyramid-building communities. They appropriated the word "white" from the Medu (known as hieroglyphs by Greeks) language and assigned it to themselves. Romans then decided to call themselves White and everyone not born in Rome, Black.

Rob Witcher published "The extended metropolis: urbs, suburbium and population," in the *Journal of Roman Archaeology* in 2005, where he wrote that Rome's population was three quarters of a million people from 27 B.C. to A.D. 100. This provides a rough idea of Rome's size for this discussion.

Rome proceeded with its conquests and invasions under the guise of Whiteness. The first people Rome targeted were in what is now modern Europe, as far north as England and Germany. These conquered people had less pigment (color) in their skin and lighter complexion than Romans, but were still considered Black by Romans.

Through conquest, invasion, slavery, and coercion, Rome grew its armies with the conquered, who then also called themselves White. Modern day notions of race stem historically from this agenda and were crystallized over time.

According to the Kemet Temples, from 80,000 B.C. until Pharaoh Akhentaton's rule in 1353 B.C., the world was living under The Great Book of Divine Ordinances, the 77 Commandments as one people. Followers of the Commandments called themselves Kem.

Understanding this, the question "Why should White people care?" becomes, "Why should the descendants of those oppressed by Rome into calling themselves White be concerned about police brutality?" The answer is for self-preservation and preserving life.

The reason why those who identify as White and participate directly, indirectly, knowingly, and unknowingly in a racist system should care about police brutality is because life is precious. Once there is agreement that life is precious, then one can go about understanding how they personally participate in racist systems that hurt others. One can then exercise power in their own spheres of influence to stop injustice, violence, and personal participation in racism. This is a long-term uphill journey.

Chapter 3

Case Study #1: 1994 Incident

The following encounter with law enforcement is a typical example of the racial profiling in policing that many Black people endure. Brandon was going home from visiting family after school. This is important because Brandon was not from the neighborhood. He was an easy target for everybody—gangs, law enforcement, whomever.

He walked through an open gate and across a parking lot on his way home. It was a regular weekday afternoon until Brandon heard screeching tires. Police cars were coming through the gate ahead of Brandon. There were one, two, then three black and white cop cars.

They rushed in and slammed on their brakes. Before the cars could come to a stop, cops were jumping out with their guns drawn. "Get on the ground!" they screamed at Brandon.

Brandon attended private school up the road. He had never been in a situation like this. But Brandon had three, four, then five guns pointed at him.

Brandon jumped to the ground. He remembers the taste of the dirt on the ground. Brandon had his arm outstretched, palms down. He did not know if he was going to die. He just begged for his life.

Brandon was with a friend, but he didn't realize his friend had stopped to use a pay phone and so didn't get caught up the way that Brandon had. Brandon was down on the ground and police were screaming commands at him. Brandon had to listen to what they were telling him. He also had to try to keep his fear in check.

Brandon remembers when the officers put him in handcuffs. They made jokes. The officers thought Brandon's name was funny and that Brandon was lying. Brandon was the only Black student admitted to College Preparatory High School, ranked top ten in the U.S.

Officers told Brandon his school didn't exist. They said that there was no school that was called College Prep, and that everything Brandon was telling them was a lie. Brandon was scared to death because these officers had guns in his face. He didn't know how to get out of this situation.

At that moment, Brandon felt helpless. He was scared. He was detained for over two hours. His friend was pretending he was on a call at a pay phone close by. The friend was a little older than Brandon, so he was already aware of his surroundings and doing the math, like, "They're about to turn [come and arrest us]." So, the friend dipped, leaving Brandon alone.

Though he was a friend, at that point, he became a witness. Brandon could see his friend, but didn't call out to him for fear of putting his life in danger. Brandon's friend did the only courageous thing he could in this situation and silently witnessed Brandon's suffering.

Somehow, Brandon's family, who were from West Oakland, got the news of what was happening to Brandon. This is where Brandon's first understanding of the jurisdictional landscape of policing began. The first lesson was what jurisdictions cover what area. What this means is that it is not enough to file a complaint and just say that "the police" did something wrong. There may be several different precincts, the county sheriff, the city police, the state police, campus police, municipal police, transit police, housing police, et al., that cover an area. If you don't know which agency was involved, it's impossible to hold someone accountable. This is when Brandon recognized the strength of having family that was from that soil, and that wherever you go, you should have someone with you from that soil. At least in a place like Oakland.

His family knew the difference between the Housing Authority, the Oakland Police Department (OPD), and the Alameda County Sheriff.

They understood which law enforcement agencies they could engage with and which they couldn't. They knew which enforcement agencies took community pressure and which didn't, and they knew which agency was detaining Brandon. Brandon's family had already-formed opinions about OPD, and they weren't afraid.

When Brandon's family found out, they showed up together on the scene and made sure that Brandon was released safely, and that nothing had happened to him while being detained. Luckily, they showed up just in time before he was taken to jail or physically hurt any further.

In that moment, Brandon understood that police may have the force but the power is and has always been with the people, if the people utilize it. Brandon saw his family show up and demonstrate in a way that led to Brandon's safe release.

Brandon's family didn't use weapons, it was just the way that they mobilized and executed that caused Brandon's release.

This is the first time of many that Brandon was profiled. Brandon had to stare down the barrels of many guns, and he never wanted his kids or anybody else's kids to have to do that. That's why he started Community Conscious Policing. So that there is a way to bring the community together with law enforcement to make a change.

Brandon was racially profiled, ridiculed, and detained, but he survived. As a survivor, and being from a place like Oakland, home to the original Black Panther Party of Self Defense and Black Lives Matter, it's Brandon's duty to stand up for those who are less fortunate and make sure there is never a similar situation again.

That's what this work is all about. It's about bringing police and community together and becoming conscious about who police serve. This is Brandon's response to make sure it doesn't happen to children like his own. Brandon takes ownership of this position. He is no longer a victim; he is a survivor.

After the incident, Brandon ran straight home, late for curfew. The incident in 1994 was important because this had never happened to him before. Brandon's mother had wondered why he was late. When Brandon told her what happened, the story was so egregious that she didn't believe him. He had done nothing wrong. Finally, after pleading an unchanging story to his mother, she believed him.

The next lesson Brandon learned is that these situations are urgent. That night, Brandon's mother put on a suit and drove him straight to OPD. Brandon and his mother filed a complaint against the police officers for what had happened.

Brandon also recognized that the system wasn't going to do anything for him and his mother. They never even heard back about that complaint. They never heard anything about it. From that point on, Brandon entered a new level of understanding at just age 14, in his freshman year in high school. He began to more fully understand popular phrases he had heard while growing up in Oakland, such as "Do for Self", "Know Thyself," and "Power to the People." These statements that spoke truth to power were made famous by leaders like Stokely Carmichael, aka Kwame Ture. Brandon was told by family and elders throughout his childhood that in Oakland, or any other place like Oakland, roughly a quarter of young Black men between the ages of 16 and 24 were victims of a homicide and about a third end up incarcerated at some point in their lives. If they survive that, then there will be racism, public health disparities, economic gaps, educational gaps, etc., waiting to be struggled through next.

By the time a young Black man starts even *looking* 16 years old, law enforcement and racist systems are trying to shove them into the school-to-prison pipeline, if they're not in it already.

The school-to-prison pipeline is the intersection of the pharmaceutical industry, Department of Education, social services, and law enforcement, which seek to profit from the movement of disadvantaged youth from classrooms to detention facilities.

This is an insider look at how the 1994 Crime Bill that former President Bill Clinton signed was then interpreted and implemented by the U.S. states. A person like Brandon was facing federal pressure from police that were basically tasked to hunt young Black men.

Chapter 4

Case Study #2: Previous Arrests as Barriers to Employment

The next incident is one that Brandon recounted on a Request for Proposal (RFP) issued by the Oregon Youth Authority (OYA). Because of this, it is important to discuss criminal records as barriers to employment.

Criminal Offenders Record Inquiry (CORI) Reform

CORI Reform is an acknowledgment that a person's criminal record is a barrier to employment, which causes poverty and promotes new crimes (Massachusetts DCJIS). This constitutes a violation of Commandment 3 from The Great Book of Divine Ordinances: "Thou shall not deprive a poor person of their subsistence."

CORI Reform in Massachusetts from 2010–2018 barred employers from asking about criminal records before a candidate is hired, limited what crimes employers and other inquirers could see on a candidate's record, limited how many years back an inquiry could see, and provided expanded access to personal inquiries to one's own criminal record. CORI reform also included provisions that automatically expunged certain minor drug offenses and allowed a person to dispute or correct errors on their records.

The state government of Massachusetts was motivated to make reforms. In June 2013, the MA Drug Lab Scandal began when disgraced chemist Annie Dookhan was charged with evidence falsification. Eventually, former state chemist Sonja Farak was also charged (Musgrave, 2019). The discovery and the subsequent 10-year investigation, which still continues as of December 21, 2020, resulted in the dismissal of more than 35,000 drug convictions (Schager, 2020).

The misconduct has cost the state more than $30 million. Compensations to the wrongfully convicted are expected to reach $10 million (Estes, 2021); payout should be in the billions to properly disincentivize this behavior from the Commonwealth of Massachusetts. During the week of December 18, 2020, Mathew Segal, the legal director for the American Civil Liberties Union of Massachusetts, said that they're still investigating "whether agencies of the Commonwealth met their duty to investigate certain lab chemists, specifically Della Saunders" (The Crime Report, 2020).

The MA Drug Lab Scandal is an example of why judging people for education, employment, housing, etc., based on criminal records is problematic and can be unjust.

On December 17, 2020, Brandon was applying for an RFP as a mentor with the Oregon Youth Authority (OYA) that involved reintegrating young adults back into their communities after being locked up.

Question two on the application asked:

"Have you ever been arrested for, convicted of, or adjudicated on any crime(s)? Yes or no? If yes, use a separate sheet of paper to list the crime(s) and describe the circumstances by which you were arrested, convicted, and/or adjudicated, and provide any information you have to help us understand why you believe your previous criminal activities will not adversely impact your ability to provide services for OYA. The explanation sheet(s) must be attached to this consent form, or it will NOT be processed."

Brandon wondered why the question didn't ask, "Have you ever been arrested as a result of police misconduct or racial profiling? If so, what was the outcome and how can we as an organization discover trauma-informed ways to prevent it from happening in our jurisdiction and facilities moving forward?" The RFP's question was traumatizing. It indicates that the state of Oregon needs CORI reform, including a comprehensive trauma-informed assessment on its policies, procedures, and practices. This would help to eliminate inadvertent harm that the state may cause through the actions of its systems and employees, such as the post-traumatic stress that was triggered by this question.

In *The New Jim Crow*, former attorney at the American Civil Liberties Union of Northern California, Michelle Alexander makes an impenetrable case illustrating how Black men age 16–24 were systemically caught up in the school-to-prison pipeline and mass incarceration during the 1980s and 1990s era of "colorblindness."

Mass incarceration is an outcome of systemic racism that targets young Black and Brown kids. Survivors of the system have to endure all the pressure from various law enforcement agencies while explaining to employers, who through their question demonstrate their ignorance of biased policing, that they should be hired. Requesting this form from Black certified clinicians, doctors, and professionals before even reviewing the application is something that they should never have to endure.

Despite this, Brandon answered "yes" to the question on the job application. He wrote about his arrest in Denton, TX.

Chapter 5

Case Study #3: Maced in the Face

2003 Denton, TX

Brandon was arrested by law enforcement in college. He was out of town supporting a scholarship fundraising event for the community with his classmates. Brandon was in the passenger's seat when the driver turned the wrong way down a one-way street as they were looking for a restaurant. There were three people in the car in total. They had worked all evening and were all sober. Unfortunately, a bicycle cop stopped them and called for backup.

Before Brandon knew it, he was maced by the officer through the driver side window. He hadn't even gotten out of the car, and he certainly hadn't done anything wrong.

It seemed like the entire police department arrived on the scene shortly thereafter, and Brandon was arrested along with two of his fraternity brothers who were in the car. They were booked, and Brandon was given very little relief from the mace in his eyes. Brandon was the only one who was maced. One cup of water was given to him for relief after his vociferous complaints.

They spent the night in jail and the car was impounded. In the holding tank, Brandon found out that he had been charged for possessing two cannabis-filled cigars that were found in the car. Even though the driver, who was the only upperclassmen with them, had pleaded no contest in a sincere attempt to take responsibility, it didn't resolve the matter for Brandon and his other fraternity brother who was in the backseat. The car didn't belong to Brandon, he was merely riding to get something to eat.

The county was still charging Brandon and his other freshman fraternity brother with possession of marijuana. If the officer could have fired mace in Brandon's face, the officer could have shot Brandon in the head for two cannabis-filled cigars had he reached for his gun rather than his mace. In a weird way, Brandon appreciates the cop now for sparing his life. In court, the prosecutor produced a large bag of cannabis that had never been in the car as evidence because the 2 cigars appeared so petty to the jury members who were missing work and family to be in court each day for trial.

Neither Brandon nor his co-defendant, who was his fraternity brother from the backseat of the car who had witnessed the entire stop, had never seen this bag of cannabis that the prosecutors had entered into evidence. This is when Brandon knew that the goal was not to discover the truth of what had occurred, but rather to send two more Black men to jail. The prosecutors appeared to be two Asian women fresh out of law school. This was a prime example of falsified evidence being used against Brandon and his fraternity brother. These are the types of incidents that Michelle Alexander expounds upon in her book, *The New Jim Crow*.

It just so happened that Brandon had been recognized as a young scholar by Washington University in St. Louis, Missouri, while in high school. He had taken his SATs in Spanish after living with host families in Spain and Mexico. His fraternity brother and codefendant was on the dean's list. They both attended Baylor University, a prestigious Southern university, and were in town supporting a fundraiser as community service for their fraternity. The step shows that Brandon and his brothers helped to produce fundraised money for Black students to attend college. They had no drugs or alcohol in their system when arrested, but none of this mattered. The police wanted them to go to jail.

The result was that Brandon was offered a plea deal, which he was encouraged to take. If he had done so, then he never would have qualified to become a faculty member and administrator in higher education. He was *not* guilty of committing a crime, and luckily, his mother is a doctor who could afford the best attorney to defend him and his brother in this small, but vibrant town.

Brandon and his co-defendant were both acquitted of all charges. They have no criminal records. All praise to the Most High, the Ancestors, Brandon's mom, the attorney, and the officers who each lined up after the verdict was read in Brandon's favor to shake Brandon's hand like gentlemen. It was a moment of respect and closure that empowered Brandon to get the hell out of town. Brandon has never returned to this day. This traumatizing story stems from the racist culture of not the individual police officers per say, but the racist culture that pervades the criminal justice system everywhere.

Chapter 6

Case Study #4: Berkeley Police Department

On this particular evening, Brandon had just arrived home after work. His mother, Sheila, was going through a divorce at the time.

Sheila and her second husband, Rick, had a court order in place from the presiding judge stating that, because of the nature of their divorce, they and Rick's son, a minor, were forbidden to enter their multimillion dollar property. The order further stated that Brandon, Sheila's son of 22 years of age, was the only resident allowed to reside at the property until the settlement of the divorce.

It just so happened that Brandon had a copy of this court order, signed by a judge, which had his name listed as the only person permitted to be on site at the property during this time.

After arriving home after work, he was taking out the trash. While he was out front, three police cars arrived. Officers got out and stopped Brandon in front of his home. He had no idea why they were there or what crime had occurred.

Officers told Brandon that they were responding to a report of a burglary, and the first officer told Brandon that "we should be able to get this cleared up rather quickly." He was a rather nice Asian man who appeared to have some experience as a police officer. However, when the second officer arrived, everything escalated. He was a Black man. Too often, Black male police officers were hardest on us as young Black men growing up, though there were other officers who were honorable and pillars in the community as well.

The officers searched Brandon's entire home, which happened to be a three-story, multi million-dollar property in the wealthy community of the Berkeley Hills in California. Brandon's family got its start in California when his grandfather owned a janitorial business that cleaned the famous Claremont Hotel in Berkeley. Because of their hard work and sacrifice, Brandon's room three generations later overlooked the same Claremont Hotel. Needless to say, searching three stories took a long time and was a waste of everyone's time. The cops seemed so determined to find something illegal to take Brandon to jail. The idea of Brandon relaxing while cooking dinner after a long day at work supporting the community was too much for the officers to mentally grasp. What detective work were they doing and who had trained them? These were random thoughts swirling through Brandon's head at the time. While officers searched the home and Brandon was detained in handcuffs, Brandon had pictures of himself with his family on the walls like any home would. It was clearly his home.

After hours of searching, officers told Brandon that he had to leave the property or go to jail. Again, he was never told what crime he was being accused of. At the time, Brandon was in shorts and a T-shirt that exposed a couple of tattoos on his arms. He had neither socks nor shoes on. He asked if he could get dressed before he left. The officers complied, and Brandon proceeded to get his own clothes out of his own room. Officers watched as Brandon dressed.

Brandon took his time and put on a suit from head to toe, complete with a tie. When he left, the black male officer asked for Brandon's keys. He told the officer that it made no sense to give a stranger the keys to his own home and that *he* would lock the door. He kept his keys, and the next morning Brandon, his mother, and her attorney filed a complaint with the Berkeley Police Review Commission (PRC), a civilian oversight board, and the Berkeley Police Department (BPD).

Brandon was confused that the officers had disobeyed a court order signed by a judge, and Brandon got to sit across from the same officers and look them in the eye as justice was being served.

During the hearing, Brandon testified and asked the civilian oversight board to close their eyes. The three-person panel composed of diverse local community members listened in silence and darkness while he explained his activities that day. He walked them through his job contributing to and upholding the community in Oakland, going to the store, preparing his meal, and getting ready for work in the morning. Then, being interrupted by police who kicked Brandon out of his own home in the cold night, with no reason and no justification.

Walking the civilian oversight board through this experience using a visualization technique, almost role-playing the event, put them in his shoes for a moment. This empowered them to center his experience as the one feeling the pain, instead of centering the experiences of the police officers. This is why Brandon not only incorporates educational, international and professional experience, but uplifts the insights that can only come from lived experience.

Brandon was granted a monetary settlement and he felt as though the officers were held accountable, even though most of the money earned in settlement went to the attorney. There were three officers involved. One passed away of natural causes before the hearing. The Asian officer received a reprimand on his record that would probably impact his ability to be promoted later. His fault was that neither he nor the other officer had intervened to stop the third officer from escalating the matter by searching Brandon's home against his will. The third officer, who happened to be a Black male in his 30s who had escalated the entire situation, was terminated from the police department for violating the police misconduct policy. While race played a role, it was not a deciding factor in the case. Diversity alone will not fix police abuse of power. The third officer had other issues prior to this formal complaint that ended up being enough reason to let him go.

Most importantly, the outcome of this case paved the way towards healing for Brandon. Without accountability, it's difficult to find healing. For this reason, Brandon does not judge anyone for how they feel as it relates to their experiences with law enforcement. There is a spectrum. Additionally, there is privilege in having access to private legal counsel and the family support to see something like this through to a peaceful resolution. For this reason,

Brandon made it his mission to support other system impacted community members in redressing situations where they felt bullied and harassed by police or private security.

The main reason that Brandon was relatively successful in this case was that he submitted a complaint to the civilian oversight board in Berkeley, where the board had been established and strengthened over the years. Brandon was able to gain some accountability there, because of the efforts of generations who had preceded him. It is important for police reform work to be in alignment with the elders and ancestors who created the opportunity to continue their legacy.

The Need for Empathy

In 1759, Adam Smith, the father of capitalism, wrote *The Theory of Moral Sentiments.* In section one, chapter one, he stated:

> "As we have no immediate experience of what other men feel, we can form no idea of the manner in which they are affected, but by conceiving what we ourselves should feel in the like situation. Though our brother is on the rack, as long as we ourselves are at our ease, our senses will never inform us of what he suffers."

Leaders who use this philosophy as justification for decisions that satisfy their fiduciary responsibility at the expense of suffering or loss of life are unacceptably wrong; this is how leaders have failed.

Science in the areas of mirror neuron research and the memory structure of water have confirmed that one can feel what others feel, and that one's health is profoundly affected by those feelings.

In the discussion about trauma or police brutality, empathy and mirror neurons must be discussed. It's important to know that the biological component of empathy is the mirror neuron system. These neurons are located in your frontal lobe and other areas of the brain. In 2005, Giacomo Rizzolatti published the article "The mirror neuron system and its function in humans," about the system that allows you to feel what another person in front of you is feeling. For example, if one eats ice cream while being watched, the observer's brain waves will "mirror" the eaters if read with an MRI.

This happens with trauma as well. When one feels fear, anger, frustration, impatience, prejudice, and aggression, these are conveyed to those nearby. In *The True Power of Water: Healing and Discovering Ourselves*, Dr. Masaru Emoto explains his studies on water also determined that negative emotions profoundly change the structure of water, damaging living systems.

Biologically, negative emotions and attitudes are felt through the mirror neurons system. If one ignores this fact, one generates or tolerates security and police officers who poison situations that require calm, stability, empathy, peace, or understanding with emotional negativity, bias, prejudice, and aggressive tendencies via the mirror neuron system.

People do have an immediate experience of what others feel. People can form an idea of the manner in which others are affected, not by conceiving but through our senses. Decision-makers must understand that preventing suffering and loss of life are pricelessly more important than their fiduciary responsibility. Leaders should feel empowered to use this understanding in this section to make and justify decisions that preserve life, even if they have a cost that must be explained.

Chapter 7

Case Study #5: Internal Affairs Department of the Oakland Police Department

On August 26, 2009, Brandon Lee spent the day studying for a Spanish teaching exam. He was set to start grad school soon. At the time, he was staying at his grandparents' home in the Oakland Hills, where he grew up. He ordered pizza to be delivered that night.

A man called Patrick drove up 30 minutes later with the pizza. Brandon signed the receipt and sat down for dinner in the TV room.

After eating, Brandon put his plate and glass in the kitchen. As he passed through the living room, he saw Patrick was still parked in front of the house.

Brandon went out and asked Patrick to leave so his grandparents could park when they arrived home from work. Patrick apologized to Brandon. Patrick had locked his keys in the delivery car. He was trying to open the car with a wire clothes hanger. Brandon immediately put on his shoes so that he could help Patrick.

Less than five minutes later, a cop car arrived with two officers. Soon after, another police car arrived with an additional officer. At first, Brandon thought Patrick had called 911 for help. That turned out not to be the case. They both explained to the officers that Brandon lived there, and that Patrick had just delivered a pizza and locked his keys in the car.

But Brandon was almost immediately handcuffed and taken to one of the police cars. When the police officers opened the door to the back seat, Brandon asked why they were putting him in the police car. They told Brandon he was being detained for trying to burglarize the delivery vehicle.

He was locked in the patrol car. Officers put Brandon back there even though he and Patrick already explained the details surrounding the locked keys. Neither of them said a burglary had taken place.

The police were able to see the name of Skyline Pizza on the young employee's T-shirt, the red pizza bag on the top of the car, and the keys in the car seat. The police officers asked Brandon for ID and he explained it was in the house. Officers said that if Brandon lived at the residence, he should have pictures hanging on the walls. Brandon stated he had many pictures in the house and told officers where they were.

Officers asked Brandon where the pizza was. He told officers the remaining portion of the pizza was in the oven. Brandon suggested that one officer could escort him into the house to retrieve his wallet and to confirm that his pictures were in the house. He told the police officers that they could go to any other residence to confirm that he lived at this house. He asked that the officers verify with Skyline Pizza that he had ordered the pizza and that Patrick had delivered the pizza to the correct address. The request to confirm his residence was ignored.

Instead of trying to confirm Brandon lived there, the police officers asked if he had any convictions or warrants. He told him, "No." They asked what he was doing at home and where his family members were. He informed the officers that he was studying for an exam and would be leaving the next day for graduate school at the School of International Training (SIT) Graduate Institute in Vermont. Even after this barrage of questions, it was clear that he was not going to be released and that the officers did not believe him.

Thankfully, one of his neighbors, Mr. Temple, came over and asked the police officers why he was in the police car. The officer asked Mr. Temple if he knew Brandon, and Mr. Temple said, "Yes."

Mr. Temple stayed and watched the officers until they opened the door and unlocked the handcuffs. The officer who'd put the handcuffs on Brandon didn't say anything. He did not apologize. Brandon asked if he was free to leave. The police officer said yes.

He asked for the officers' names and badge numbers. They did not want to give them out. Instead, they wanted to explain their actions.

One officer asked Brandon to sit in the other police car so he could explain, but Brandon was afraid, and told them he would not sit in the police car.

They wanted to show Brandon the call that had come through dispatch on their computer monitor alerting them to a burglary in progress.

Spider Sickness

At this point it's important to press pause on this story and digress to discuss "spider sickness," its meaning, and its relevance to the current discussion about police brutality. There is a Chiricahua (Apache) prophecy that was spoken by Stalking Wolf who was born in the 1870s. This prophecy was recounted at the Maine Primitive Skills School in 2009 by Michael Douglass (Douglass, 2010).

The prophecy states that people will be cut off from the Earth because they have forgotten the old ways (how to live in harmony with nature). They will bring boxes of fire into their homes. They will be mesmerized by the dancing lights from the boxes of fire, and the box will take their minds. The boxes will make them do things and they will become like zombies and obey the box. This is the spider sickness that will creep across the land. As the sickness spreads, cities (urban infrastructure) will begin to fall. This will become worse as technology fails. The spider sickness will make zombie wars where brothers will kill and eat each other in crumbling cities. Those that cling to technology will not make it. Those who remember the ways of the Earth (indigenous wisdom) and leave technology will be the only ones to survive.

The boxes of fire are electric boxes: iPhones, Androids, TVs, movie screens, computers, display screens, video games, virtual reality, radar screens, Hollywood productions, missile guidance system screens, radios, medical device screens, and in this case, a police dispatch computer monitor in a police car.

Officers assumed the dispatch monitor was correct (it was not), hand-cuffed Brandon, and put him in a cage designed to hold people, all because of a few words on a monitor. How many police killings started the same way, because a *digital display screen* was incorrect? Society and law enforcement must do better. People have to use and trust their own brains, even if the police dispatch monitor says there's a suspect. People, and especially law enforcement officers, have to use their own senses, reasoning, and logic because the monitor is incapable of knowing whether it speaks the truth.

Case Study Continued

Back to Brandon's story.

The officers wanted to show him the dispatch of a burglary call on their computer monitor. This didn't matter to Brandon, because he had told the officers to knock on the door of any neighbor to prove his innocence. His neighbors would have told the police that Brandon's family had lived in this house for four generations, and that he had lived there himself for decades. As a result of officers ignoring his request, Brandon's detainment lasted a couple of hours until his friend's father came out of their home, spoke to the officers, and demanded that Brandon be released. Their "investigation" had gotten in the way of kids coming home from school (the officers had the entire street blocked off) and was simply embarrassing for his neighbors to watch. Two police cars, each on the middle of their respective side of the street, blocked traffic in both directions on this two-lane residential cul de sac.

It was painful for Brandon to be accused of burglarizing his own home. It's an upper-income neighborhood. Brandon was a college graduate, bilingual, and in graduate school. He was home studying. Obviously, no laws had been broken, and he was not arrested. Nothing remains on his record from this police stop, but the trauma still lingers and informs his work to this day.

The officers decided not to believe Brandon. They were not protecting Brandon's home or himself. Brandon is afraid to think of what could have happened if his neighbor had not arrived on the scene.

In light of what happened to Brandon in front of his own home, Brandon submitted a letter of complaint to the Internal Affairs Department of the Oakland Police Department on August 19, 2010. Danielle Outlaw, who is currently Police Commissioner for the Philadelphia Police Department, was the director of OPD Internal Affairs, which handles such complaints.

Brandon should not have been detained and any competent police officer should have been able to figure out Brandon lived there. Those actions damaged the relationship between officers, Brandon, his family, and his neighbors. Brandon thought their behavior should have been classified as harassment.

Unfortunately, the Oakland Police Department's IAD supported the officers and denied Brandon's claim of police misconduct. His complaint a few years prior against the Berkeley Police Department had been upheld by the Police Review Commission when Brandon had been detained in front of his mother's home in the Berkeley Hills.

The difference in how BPD and OPD handled his complaint motivated Brandon to go public with his story. Every morning before class at SIT in Vermont, Brandon would send his story to influencers in the media and grassroots community organizations, eventually hundreds of them, who were leading the fight against police brutality and politicians.

On March 7, 2011, Brandon testified at Oakland City Hall. Out of the three people invited by Rashida G., a prominent Oakland activist, and People United for a Better Life in Oakland (PUEBLO) , Brandon was the only one to show up that day. Rashida G., and PUEBLO helped Brandon submit a City of Oakland Citizens Complaint Review Form for the record.

One field on the form asked, "Were you injured? NO OR YES (Describe)" Brandon checked "yes" citing Post-Traumatic Stress Disorder (PTSD) as his injury. The next question asked, "What would you like as a result of this complaint?" Brandon wrote "SHUT DOWN INTERNAL AFFAIRS. Disciplinary action/ CPRB should take over citizen complaints." It was about getting Brandon's testimony on record, which is what Rashida and PUEBLO needed to help him and so many other families.

On March 9, 2011, the American Civil Liberties Union of Northern California wrote a letter of support on his behalf and on behalf of the Coalition of Police Accountability (formerly known as PUEBLO).

On June 30, 2011, Oakland Mayor Jean Quan cast the deciding vote to take the Internal Affairs Department's (IAD) **$1,468,158** budget and use it to fund the Civilian Police Review Board. In Oakland, Brandon supported grassroots efforts led by PUEBLO, a nonprofit organization, to fund the Civilian Oversight of Police Board (CPRB). They found the IAD incompetent through Brandon's formal complaint using data collected by PUEBLO, his testimony on record at the civilian police review board, and the support of ACLU Northern California, to propose the reallocation funds from IAD to the community led CPRB.

The City of Oakland's Measure LL, which was the result of these collective efforts, was passed in 2016 (Ballotpedia, 2016). It amended the city charter to establish a civilian commission to oversee the police. The commission has the power to investigate police misconduct and can fire the Chief of Police, as well as recommend any candidates for the office. Measure LL became one of the strongest CPRBs in the country and is now the Police Commission and Community Police Review Agency. It also has the power to hold evidentiary hearings and review OPD's confidential records.

Brandon is proud to have played a role in what is now one of the strongest civilian oversight of police boards in the country. When people speak of "abolishing" or "defunding" the police, they are looking to redirect funds that are wasted on law enforcement to efforts that will empower the community to respond to its own issues.

This is an example of Popular Education, a term coined by educator and philosopher Paulo Freire (AFSC, 2021), or a public-health centered response model, to end unnecessary and unintended law enforcement violence. Brandon's experience shows how one person's complaint can become the straw that breaks the back of systemic racist practices, such as profiling. Community Conscious Policing looks like communities having systemic power and influence as taxpayers over their police departments, including hiring, promotion, termination, tactics, discipline, and training of police chiefs and their subordinates. Measures that don't include this shift of power are a part of the problem.

This Oakland case study shows how one community member can tap into communal resources and wisdom. Doing so resulted in police accountability and led to local legislation that could greatly reduce the risk of systemic profiling and law enforcement violence. This study also demonstrates how partnering with everyone from local grassroots and national advocacy groups to social media influencers and media outlets is key to raising the awareness of individual instances or patterns of racial profiling. Brandon would like to especially acknowledge the Coalition of Police Accountability for their unwavering support and leadership during a very difficult time in his life.

Chapter 8

Case Study #6: Formal Complaint against a Telecom Company

Hillsborough, Oregon, December 31, 2019, 11:07 PM EST.

On December 31, Brandon's wife Hun Taing, a Chinese-Cambodian genocide survivor, went to the AT&T store to complain about services and fees that were added to her bill without consent. The store manager and an employee treated his wife with the utmost disrespect.

They did not pull up her account to provide any assistance, but rather accused her of being rude. When she came home and shared with Brandon that she had been hustled and then kicked out of the store, they packed their kids up and went back together.

Upon arrival, Brandon witnessed the disrespectful tone and attitude of the manager personally. When Brandon told the manager, "I need to file a complaint," the manager refused to share any information that would help to redress the situation.

Instead, the manager called the police on Brandon in front of his face and reported that there was an "irate" customer who wouldn't agree to leave the premises when asked. Brandon had not raised his voice. He had not cursed or used expletive language. He had not violated any policies.

What triggered the manager to call 911 was Brandon calling the manager incompetent at his job. As a faculty member who had taught Harvard Business case studies to international professionals earning their master's degrees in Business Administration (MBA), Brandon was more than qualified to make this assessment.

Brandon was dressed impeccably in a nice suit. It's a shame that it even has to be said, but how one dresses can have a real impact on how people respond to each other in this classist country. "Classist" means that something is stratified or separated into a hierarchy determined by prejudice and discrimination based on socio-economic status.

In this case, the manager was intimidated intellectually and realized he was not equipped for the conversation. He could not answer Brandon's questions, and then, all of a sudden, his bias turned into a discriminatory act when he decided to call the police.

The manager lied, in a store full of people, when he said that Brandon was "irate" and had refused to leave the store. What the manager had failed to report was that he was the manager who had authorized his sales associate to "slam and cram" Hun with fees and services that she had not asked for. Slam and cram is when customers are signed up for things they didn't ask for at costs that weren't fully disclosed.

This is what Brandon alleged. It was based upon strict examination of his records, informal interviews with other store employees, and the company's executive leadership, who were very helpful overall. The associate who had "helped" Hun initially and caused all of this confusion has since moved to Hawaii, and probably got as much money from her as possible before he left. Hun was taken care of in the end. She and Brandon changed phone companies after they were compensated.

The couple were able to demonstrate that the manager approved the initial transaction and was therefore complicit. This manager responded in a racist way by calling the police to do his dirty work.

He thought that he could simply hustle Brandon's wife as an easy target, treat her poorly, and then dismiss them. It won't work that way in 2021. It's important to note that the phone line was for a minority-owned business, and that there should be laws in place to protect people against big companies trying to exploit small businesses and then turn a blind eye to the abuse. In the end, they were able to move on, unlike so many others who have lost their lives and livelihoods in situations when the police were summoned.

Brandon filed a complaint with the Federal Communication Commission (FCC), which handles complaints about telecom providers like AT&T. They mediated between Brandon and the office of the president of this global company. The telecom company did everything Brandon asked for, which included major cost reductions in the couple's monthly bill and disciplinary actions against the store manager and participants in the scam.

The CEO "resigned" after less than a year in the position, apparently related to other circumstances, but you never know which complaint was the tipping point.

In his heart, Brandon knew that he did what was necessary to ensure that no other community member was subject to the same discrimination that he faced, at least in that store. To give credit where it is due, the sheriff's office did not respond when the manager called.

It took many steps to bring accountability in this case. Brandon filed a Better Business Bureau (BBB) complaint. He researched the store's ranking and discovered that it was low. He also could read other complaints to discover a pattern or practice.

Next, Brandon filed a Yelp review. Yelp.com is a website that crowdsources business reviews online. He researched the store's ranking and discovered that it was low here too. He discovered a pattern. Brandon's work in public policy, combined with a racial equity perspective, helped him in this analysis.

Between the negative BBB and Yelp reviews, he gleaned themes from independent reviews from customers. The themes that emerged from this qualitative data provided by the narratives of the stories, along with the quantitative data of the actual numerical scores that previous customers had used to rank the telephone company's services, they all matched what he felt about the store, which was located in Beaverton, Oregon.

In Oregon, victims of biased phone calls to the police, like the store manager made, are able to sue the caller for up to $250 under an Act Relating to Unlawfully Summoning a Police Officer, HB-3216, a measure overwhelmingly approved by the state legislature on June 6, 2019 (Oregon Legislative Information, 2020). This law states, "A person may bring a civil action for damages against any person who knowingly causes a police officer to arrive at a location to contact another person with the intent to infringe on their constitutional rights; unlawfully discriminate against them; cause them to feel harassed, humiliated or embarrassed; cause them to be expelled from somewhere they have a right to be; or damage their reputation or economic interests; the harmed party may seek justice in civil court." It is up to the discretion of the court whether a fine would be assessed in this particular case, because although the police officer was summoned, they did not arrive.

Brandon was able to make the connection between the manager's prejudiced beliefs about minority groups and how he discriminated against the couple based on these beliefs and then attempted to use his privilege to bully them into submission or dismissal.

Hun felt dismissed by the manager. Brandon felt the same way. Many other customers reported feeling the same way within the prior three months. At this point, Brandon's complaint was an indicator of systemic issues, and escalated all the way to the office of the president.

Brandon's federal complaint could have been a factor in why the CEO "resigned." Brandon will never know, and that's beside the point. This case study is an example of how one motivated customer can cause a whole lot of problems for an institution, especially if a racial equity policy is not embedded in the fabric of the organization.

Not only could this oversight cost people their jobs and livelihoods, it can stop billion-dollar mergers from happening down the line, if the company survives at all. In 2014, Michael McCauley and Christopher Casey wrote that the federal government stopped the merger of two corporate giants because of customer service-related issues in the consumer report, "The Comcast/Time Warner Cable Merger: A Bad Deal for Consumers."

Some people ask why Brandon didn't sue for more damages or punitive penalties for how they were mistreated. He has been through too many of these scenarios, and he'd rather stand on the pillars of spiritual practice and continue working instead.

Personally, Brandon wanted to correct the wrong, to be made whole. Once he achieved this objective, he transitioned to compassion, mercy, and the search for true justice, where Brandon's trauma doesn't turn him into a perpetrator of violence. It's a thin line.

Hun felt compensated and heard. She felt good about the accountability that came as a result, and Brandon was satisfied that what happened to him would never happen to someone else, at least in their area, for the foreseeable future. They were able to then begin healing from what they had endured. All he cared about was Hun feeling empowered and victorious! The rest, he could let go of.

At least, he's working on it.

Chapter 9

Communication That Benefits People

In 2015, Brandon was the Retention and Multicultural Center Coordinator for his community college. As soon as he got hired, the assistant coordinator, who had been a Black male, the office assistant, who was Latina, and Brandon's boss, who was also Latina, all left the college.

Very quickly, Brandon found himself in a job that he knew was not going to be sustainable, because the three people of color around him had left as soon as he came on board.

The students and Brandon's colleagues were great, but he had a pretty tough experience as the only Black administrator because of tokenism. Brandon was looking for his next job, so he went to a fairly well-known event in Portland called "Say Hey." The event occurs once a month to introduce new Black people in town to the local Black community, because there aren't many Black people in Portland.

Brandon attended and announced that T4T had conducted a local police training and they were preparing to conduct statewide training with the FBI National Academy of Associates.

While standing in line, Brandon saw a well-dressed gentleman in a suit similar to his own. Brandon thought maybe he was a fellow fraternity brother, so he went and introduced himself. He wasn't a fraternity member, but he seemed to be in a similar line of work.

Devin James owned a company called the Devin James Group (DJG), a public relations firm whose motto was, "Communication Benefits People." It is different from what T4T does in terms of racial equity, organizational development, and executive coaching. T4T is in the cultural paradigm shifting business. With T4T, improvements in public relations and positive press will occur, but they are earned rather than purchased directly. DJG, by contrast, is a public relations firm.

Devin was very smart, younger than Brandon, but very successful in business. Devin was recognized in Black Enterprise, a premiere US Black business magazine. Devin was established. However, Devin's primary base of operations was in the midwestern US, which is very different from the West Coast. Brandon discovered that Devin had been working on promoting businesses and entrepreneurship in St. Louis when the police killing in Ferguson occurred along with community uprisings.

Since Devin was already in town, the city of Ferguson had asked him to support them during the community uprisings. Devin had spent some time incarcerated in the past. He had defended himself during a home invasion and an assailant lost their life. As a result, Devin did go to prison for a short time, but he lived to tell the story. Devin is a Black man who had been impacted by the prison industrial complex and then transformed his life into doing public relations. Therefore, Ferguson at one time regarded him as an asset and hired him as their consultant.

There are some important lessons Brandon learned from his experiences while working as a consulting partner with DJG. First, the role of public relations when it comes to police–community relations—how a story is told, how it's depicted, and the images that are shown can amplify or help a situation. If a person is not skilled in racial equity, doesn't have the educational background or a track record in racial equity work, if they haven't done cultural paradigm shifts or been a grassroots organizer, then they skip those steps and try to promote an image of reconciliation without actual repair having taken place, the situation is going to get worse.

This is what Brandon discovered first hand after working closely with

Devin. To Devin's credit, Ferguson was not what Devin had come to St. Louis to do. Devin did what most Black men probably would have done if they were called upon in that situation; he stepped up to be of service. However, Brandon knew that if you don't bring those aforementioned skills to the table, then public relations can amplify an already polarized situation.

Devin traveled to Oregon right after the community uprising in Ferguson. At the "Say Hey" event, Brandon found out Devin worked in Ferguson, and he was fascinated because he had just done work with Corvallis PD and had a contract to do T4T training on a statewide level. Devin had experience in Ferguson, doing something similar to T4T, so Brandon invited Devin to join him, to make introductions for Devin and to allow Brandon an opportunity to learn from a mentor.

Devin came on board and delivered the keynote at T4T's state training. T4T started with law enforcement in the morning, then a community group came in for lunch. Right before they broke for lunch to bring in the community, Devin delivered his keynote speech to law enforcement.

It was an awful speech. Devin used profanity, among other blunders. Brandon couldn't understand how someone with Devin's credentials, who had done work of this level in Ferguson, could miss the mark so drastically.

That was a sign that Brandon needed to stop looking outside of himself for answers. They got through the experience and the FBINAA were very honest about their feedback regarding Devin. The FBINAA were very supportive of Brandon, Hun, and the other facilitators.

Brandon learned a couple of things through this experience. There was a video done in Ferguson of the police chief apologizing to the family of Michael Brown who was killed by Officer Darren Wilson. It was done in a stale studio environment, and it wasn't received well in the community. That was Devin's idea. Devin also had the Ferguson police chief go out with the protestors, even though protestors were protesting against the chief. Things like this were almost taunting the protestors and the victim's family. Brandon knows that these actions weren't intended to be harmful, but if one doesn't have the correct experience in racial equity and training, then actions usually result in fueling the flames of unrest, mistrust, and trauma in the community.

Chapter 10

From Accountability to Training

After Brandon was detained unlawfully for burglarizing his own home where he had lived with his mother in the Berkeley hills, Brandon was awarded a monetary settlement that resulted in disciplinary actions against the officers involved. Most people would have stopped here, but Brandon knew that he couldn't, because he still didn't feel safe. Police accountability in Oakland may have improved, but nothing had changed elsewhere.

From 2013 to 2015, Brandon was the NAACP legal redress committee chairman, which allowed him to advocate for others' civil rights. Brandon was also an Oregon State University faculty member and director of the center for fraternity and sorority life.

Brandon knew what steps were necessary to take a personal complaint of police misconduct all the way to changing local legislation and reallocating money from police budgets to fund community-focused initiatives. Community Conscious Policing is a public health response model to end law enforcement violence that includes, but is not limited to, shifting resources from police departments to community-based solutions.

These solutions include: more comprehensive addiction services; reintegration programs after incarceration; resources to support survivors of domestic and sexual abuse; decriminalizing mental health; reintegrating counselors and Black teachers into schools; making sure police from the community are thoroughly trained in de-escalation; hiring patrols that do not rely on carrying lethal weapons to do their jobs, engaging with neighbors and local residents through a racial equality lens, and fully funding the infrastructure needed to support people without homes.

It became overwhelmingly clear, with the support of Hun, that Brandon's purpose at this time is to write this book and introduce the Community Conscious Policing model to the world.

In Ferguson, Missouri, in August 2015, an unarmed Black teen, Michael Brown, was killed by a police officer. In Baltimore, Maryland, April 2015, Freddie Gray died handcuffed in the back of a police van according to Sari Horwitz, Mark Berman, and Wesley Lowery who wrote "Sessions Orders Justice Dept. Review of All Police Reform Agreements, Including Ferguson" for the Washington Post in an article published April 3, 2017 (Horowitz, et al., 2017). There were community uprisings in several major cities, including Baltimore, as the country nervously waited to hear if officer Darrin Wilson would be charged in the death of Michael Brown. MSNBC reported protests over Freddie Gray's murder commenced on April 29, 2015, in Denver, San Diego, and New York City. They also reported Freddy Gray protests in Philadelphia and Cincinnati on April 30, 2015 (Ortiz, 2015).

After the state of emergency in Ferguson (Swaine, 2015) and martial law in Baltimore (Stolberg, 2015), Hun and Brandon sought ways to support the students by establishing a dialogue with local police to confront biases and rebuild a shared vision of community.

Brandon supported students by facilitating "Know Your Rights" training and role-plays, connecting them with the NAACP, assisting them with filing complaints, connecting African students to the local Black community, and helping students relocate when threatened with violence at their apartment. He wanted to create a workshop to engage authentically and build understanding between students and police. "Authentically" means a genuine effort as opposed to superficial or perfunctory one.

Tony Cheng writes in "Input without Influence: The Silence and Scripts of Police and Community Relations" (2019) that perfunctory policing can be seen "where officers superficially comply with procedural requirements of a program or practice, but resist substantive changes in performance—leaving residents to shoulder the consequences of police inaction."

Protecting survivors' identities is an authentic action that benefits the community. Speaking to people in their native language, or meeting potential participants in their own neighborhoods to reduce transportation cost and give participants "home-field advantage" (the familiarity, comfort, and security of home as opposed to a courthouse, police station, office, etc.) are all steps that tell potential participants they can speak to cops safely in Brandon and Hun's forum.

There were guidelines: no guns, no uniforms, and all meetings were facilitated by a survivor of police misconduct with educational and professional experience in legal redress, facilitation, and reconciliation.

While law enforcement leadership contributed to the workshop, ultimately it was a space designed by community members that centered the experiences of people most impacted by law enforcement violence. Historically, this would include Black people (men, women, women of transgender experience), Native women, Latinx families, Southeast Asian communities, people in recovery, neighbors experiencing houselessness or mental health crises, the disabled community, immigrants, and refugees, to name just a few.

Brandon settled his lawsuit against the Berkeley PD in 2006 for police misconduct that resulted in disciplinary actions against the officers involved. The next step was to volunteer in support of grassroots-led organizations that funded what has become one of the strongest community police review agencies in the nation. At the NAACP, the job of legal redress chairman involves supporting community members who have been the victims of racial profiling and police misconduct. Hun served as the executive director of the NAACP Corvallis–Albany branch. Brandon had also served as a board member on the Law Enforcement Data Collection and Policy Review Committee (LECC) in Oregon, moving his skills to the state level.

Oregon LECC

The LECC, now referred to as Equity in Policing, was the task force put together by the governor's office under the leadership of the Oregon Attorney General until a scandal broke out. Two influential people who

Brandon served with on the LECC with were Dr. Brian Renauer, Director of the Criminal Justice Policy Research Institute at Portland State University, and Captain Sam Kamkar, who led the subcommittee of the LECC on revamping law enforcement training curriculum statewide to include an equity lens for the Department of Public Safety Standards and Training.

The people leading implicit bias training efforts for law enforcement statewide in 2016 during community uprisings nationwide in response to police-involved killings—or lynchings as some would call them—were Sam Kamkar and Attorney General Rosenbaum, who leads the state's efforts against hate crimes for the Oregon Department of Justice. Brandon provided feedback to the LECC Annual Report 2016 when he served as a committee member, and many of his suggestions were incorporated into the final edit.

The LECC is a governor-appointed committee that partnered with Portland State University. HB2355: Chapter 706, effective date August 15, 2017, is the Oregon law that was written as a result of the work done by the LECC while Brandon served as a member. House Bill 2355 directed the Oregon Criminal Justice Commission to develop a method for recording data concerning officer-initiated pedestrian and traffic stops (The Oregonian, 2017). The law mandated that all police officers in Oregon collect data on a person's perceived race, ethnicity, age, and sex during pedestrian and traffic-stops. This makes Oregon the second state, after California, to record this data.

The data accrued through HB 2355 is reviewed by the Oregon Criminal Justice Commission to identify patterns or practices of profiling. The commission reports its findings annually to the governor and the Department of Public Safety Standards and Training. The legislation requires police to complete training in cultural competency and implicit bias to prevent profiling. It also reclassified narcotic possession from a felony to a misdemeanor.

Brandon is not sure what the LECC has done since he stepped down. Other task forces have been put together to tackle similar issues, and they consist of the same professionals as before most times. Part of the reason Brandon stepped down from the LECC was the lack of meaningful community engagement and in 2017, for example, zero complaints made by diverse community residents who complained against police in Oregon were found to be validated or upheld by the LECC. T4T could do better independently in police accountability, law enforcement training, community oversight of police, and healing from the trauma of law enforcement violence.

Brandon knows that accountability will not result from these types of task forces and committees, because they don't consist of diverse community members who are the actual survivors of law enforcement violence. It's through this LECC task force process that Brandon truly understood the inadequacy in police training statewide, which he had already critiqued from a racial equity perspective as a survivor of racial profiling a year prior while preparing for the initial Community Conscious Policing Workshop in Corvallis.

Corvallis PD was the only law enforcement organization that had been submitting their stop data (traffic stops) for review to the LECC, an "objective" third party, to determine if racial bias was detected in their police stops during the past five years. Brandon was able to demonstrate based on the statistical data provided that a drastic increase of stops in the "other race" category in 2011 indicated a need for a deeper probe to determine if racial profiling indeed existed outside of Asian, White, Black, and Latino race categories. To discover more answers, there was a need for qualitative data in the form of actual stories from the ground in Corvallis by people who were being most impacted by these traffic stops to get a clearer view of what the statistics were revealing.

This group of researchers, police leaders, and lawyers on the LECC couldn't see the types of insights that Brandon brought to the committee from actually living and working in Corvallis. This is when Brandon discovered that having a White man as the primary researcher analyzing stop data for racial profiling only perpetuates racism. It's also problematic for these same White men and White police officers to be teaching "bias" training that has proven to be ineffective and a waste of taxpayer dollars. It's all about the money, rather than employing the best talent to solve each problem. According to Portland Police Bureau's listening sessions in 2006, even the community had asked that PPB employ Black, Indigenous, and people of color as police trainers, especially as it related to training about implicit bias and racial profiling.

Chapter 11

Law Enforcement Data Collection and Policy Review Committee

B randon evaluated and reviewed the LECC Annual Report, prior to the final draft being submitted to the Oregon legislature in 2016.

"Some Other Race"

Brandon thought that the Corvallis Police Department Data Collection was fine, except for a few community considerations. Specifically, the classification of "some other race," and extreme cases involving CPD stopping Black men in Corvallis.

Brandon's family, who is multiethnic, plurilingual and biracial, could be classified by an officer as "some other race." It's probably why none of Brandon's law enforcement stops registered as "bias" on someone's data chart until he sat on the LECC, successfully sued law enforcement, or filed a complaint resulting in disciplinary actions.

Since this classification "some other race" was so large and consistently growing in the number of stops every year on the annual report, but was also the category the LECC knew the least about, Brandon was concerned that cultural incompetence may have played a role in how the LECC collected data.

Brandon evaluated the data through his agency T4T. In addition, T4T conducted regular site visits, participated on oral board interviews, and conducted community/student surveys. They reviewed hundreds of evaluations submitted by both CPD and community members who participated together in T4T training.

The Corvallis data by itself in the LECC annual report seemed skewed to represent only a Eurocentric, dominant-culture narrative. It's dangerous for community members that the "some other race" category had been skyrocketing upward over the years. It indicated to Brandon that bias may have been present but the attention of law enforcement could have shifted from race to class.

As a result of the classification "some other race," one can simply infer but not actually discover what residents are being impacted most by traffic stops in Corvallis. "Some other race" represents a big number of Corvallis residents, and it's unfortunate that this category was not disaggregated into more relevant cultural themes or races.

In 2011, the International Living Learning Center (INTO) at Oregon State University opened, which brought in thousands of international students from all around the world to learn English and attend OSU. Many ESL students came from countries like Saudi Arabia and received a government salary for attending, or from China with a lot of private money.

They often bought brand-new fast cars right off the lot. Some of them raced back in their home countries and others had never driven in the US before. Some students even abandoned their expensive cars in the parking lot when they returned home.

Brandon assumed that many ESL students living at INTO OSU may have been pulled over around campus and Corvallis, which may explain the climb of "some other race" on the data chart, not to mention other migrants, immigrants, and refugees who arrived in the broader community.

As Director of Greek Life, Brandon received every police report that occurred on or near campus regarding Oregon State University fraternities and student clubs. He worked closely with student conduct and the Office of Equity and Inclusion. Racial intimidation and bias almost always went unpunished, if it was even addressed at that time. Brandon saw the university blame survivors for hate crimes, rather than report them to police for assistance in finding the perpetrator.

Sexual assaults and domestic violence were hardly ever solved or prosecuted, unless the aggressor was a Black man. Therefore, the data collected by CPD didn't represent community voice. This needed to be acknowledged in some capacity.

For example, Brandon was referred to as "colored" by a high-ranking Corvallis officer who oversaw training and officer discipline. He didn't even know that he had made a blunder, which impacted Brandon for days later. None of these types of encounters or conversations are represented in the stop data collected.

Without qualitative stories to supplement the data, the numbers don't say much and don't help those who need it most. It is imperative that the community be allowed to share directly their experience with any department that LECC evaluated and be represented somehow, before LECC, as a committee, recommended a label as definite as "no bias detected."

In Brandon's opinion, it was necessary to unpack the "some other race" category and include qualitative data from all marginalized communities in Corvallis before it could be concluded that there was "no bias detected in the Corvallis Police Department stop data collected over the previous five years." The entire data collection classification system needed to be updated to be more inclusive of current communities so that training, etc., could be tailor-made to fit.

Brandon was never personally stopped by Corvallis PD. It's very possible that race does not play a role in who gets stopped there. However, it is very possible that race played a role when an officer pulled a gun on a young Black man riding his bike through OSU's campus.

"Wynne says he was riding his bicycle to go work out when Officer Teeter pulled up in an SUV, got out of the vehicle and pointed his gun at Wynne. Corvallis police have said Teeter was responding to a federal warrant for 38-year-old Sylvester Cortez Harrison, of Albany. The warrant included "cautionary indicators" of "violence and a weapon."

"They said it has nothing to do with race? It definitely did," Wynne said. "How do you confuse five-five with five-ten? It's not necessary at all to pull a gun unless you know...(BRUTTELL Corvallis Gazette-Times - Sep 9, 2015)"

Wynne went directly to the news after this incident with Officer Teeter, but luckily for Jon Sassaman, the Corvallis police chief, Brandon was able to avoid the police getting sued. For Wynne, it's likely he may not have won in court. Even if he had, police departments often have insurance that pays out lawsuits that rarely result in an organizational culture shift for the better. However, the headlines alone would have caused some damage to CPD in the court of public opinion if this case had continued. What Wynne did receive from trusting Brandon and his Legal Redress Committee of the local NAACP branch was the opportunity to speak directly with the police chief and tell him what changes he wanted to see in officers' conduct and why. Wynne also received a sincere apology directly from the chief that served as a stepping stone toward reconciliation moving forward. This traumatic experience transformed into an opportunity for growth and healing. The chief gave his word that the officer involved would be held accountable for his actions and retrained.

In another case, the NAACP Corvallis/Albany Branch had to intervene on behalf of a Black male student who had recently graduated from OSU. His mom sought us out after another attorney took her money without rendering services. The young man was charged excessively in our opinion. What bothered Brandon most about both cases is that neither of them resulted in a training or learning opportunity for CPD officers.

This was a pivotal moment, especially in light of Black men being killed on camera every week during the time. With African Americans being such a small population in Corvallis, the NAACP began to pay more attention to how they were treated once they were stopped.

Student surveys from the African Student Association reported police following Black students with a light flashing on them or asking them to leave a certain area of town. These incidents, for example, would not be reported as a stop.

In CPD's defense, those surveyed did not recall which specific agency had made the transgression. After the training, Lieutenant Jim Zessin retired.

Trainer Nick Hurley accepted a training position at the Department of Public Safety Standards and Training. Now, he is the current Chief of Police for the Corvallis Police Department. T4T decided that it was time to go another direction for their company. The new leadership at the time was not as focused on centering the experiences of the community who were most impacted by law enforcement violence and profiling. The Black police officer who was hired shortly after T4T's participation on the oral review boards, Community Conscious Policing workshops, and Legal Redress Committee work with NAACP Corvallis/Albany Branch also retired. This case study with CPD is an example of racial equity work, civic engagement with diverse communities, confronting biases, and rebuilding a shared vision of community that needs to be properly funded in order to be sustainable. Based on the evaluations, which included both community and cops, the feedback was overwhelmingly in favor of more opportunities like our Community Conscious Policing Workshops to engage proactively as a means to prevent unfortunate circumstances from occurring in the future.

Another question that arose during the LECC stop data collection process was raised about African and Middle Eastern students who are classified as White. An officer may identify the student as "other race" on their data collection if the person doesn't self-identify. These misperceptions, lack of cultural competence, and colonial checkboxes regarding race also impacts the data collected.

International students, particularly learning English as a second language, wouldn't file a complaint if they felt their civil rights had been violated. Brandon often found these students had been taken advantage of in their lease agreements and were sometimes harassed in the community. Stop data isn't the only way to determine bias in an agency. What should have been more heavily considered was community input from Corvallis residents, particularly from those who fit the "some other race" criteria.

As so many complaints were filed during the same time with the LECC and his branch of the NAACP, Brandon wanted to know who was being impacted most by traffic stops and how many times were officers being held accountable? This information would help Brandon understand a more holistic view. He wanted to know how easy it was for community members to access and submit a complaint for residents in Corvallis to the LECC. He also wanted to know who sat on the citizen police review board for Corvallis PD, how they were selected, and what was their track record of holding officers accountable?

Brandon asked whether the LECC was training the community in Oregon on how to file complaints? He wanted to know how the LECC planned on meeting in locations that were more accessible to the communities who were most impacted by racial profiling and police misconduct. Brandon worked with CPD, but he didn't even know where or how to find a complaint form if needed after a traffic stop.

The Oregon Chapter of the NAACP Legal Redress Committee handled two pretty big cases where African American men were treated far more extremely than necessary by CPD. Jon Sassaman and then-Captain Jim Zessin drove to Beaverton at Brandon's request to talk about it. For that, Brandon gives them credit. There is no doubt these two officers cared deeply about their work and community. They have both since retired, and T4T thanks them for their invitation to host our first Community Conscious Policing Workshop.

Reasons why stops labeled "some other race" had increased so significantly over time needed to be discovered, the classification itself needed to be broken down into more inclusive categories, and training needed to be offered with a more culturally relevant curriculum to help officers decipher who they are serving and how best to serve and protect them.

Brandon's feedback for the 2016 LECC Annual Report also questioned the report's statement that, "The overall decline in stops and the decline for two larger racial/ethnic categories indicate reduced risk for biased policing over time in Corvallis." The "some other race" classification consistently rose over time in the data, so Brandon questioned if the LECC was really able to make that statement with confidence. African Americans are such a small population in Corvallis, it seemed that bias had shifted to rich international students who were relatively easy targets instead. They were in the United States to learn English and most likely would not challenge anyone in authority, such as a police officer over a traffic ticket.

It demonstrated, at the very least, that some cultural proficiency training was necessary to help officers better engage residents who may have recently moved to Corvallis and updated reporting categories to meet this new shift in population. Who amongst the law enforcement trainers had recent experience being racially profiled in the last six months in Oregon?

Brandon thought the LECC should consider diversifying its training staff and include more community members who are qualified to train law enforcement. Multiethnic and multilingual training teams are essential in the 21st century.

Brandon asked why LECC didn't engage the Corvallis community directly in order to get their perspective and provide a more balanced, holistic view of the reported data? The statistics should be complemented with Community Conscious Policing Workshops or something that provides a way for impacted Black, Indigenous, and other communities of color to speak in their own voice. Sometimes the feedback for law enforcement is positive too.

Brandon needed to be a part of every aspect of training and curriculum design with LECC–DPSST based on what he saw as a committee member. He didn't really trust that they could do it without an agency like T4T. Brandon thought the in-service training, hiring of trainers, and curriculum design all needed to be monitored by an independent 3rd party. T4T was one of the few community-led organizations with the lived, educational and professional experience and track record to serve in this capacity.

The problem Brandon found consistently was that hate crimes and sexual assaults went unsolved most of the time on or around campus at Oregon State University during this time. Rarely would the Campus or Corvallis Police catch the perpetrator. Rarely were these incidents even reported, which is what inspired Brandon to leave higher education and publish this book. Even Brandon was called a "n****r" on campus during his doctoral program, but no one was ever held responsible after he reported the incident to the Office of Diversity, Equity, and Inclusion. The LECC, similar committees and task forces, must become more inclusive of community voices that center diverse residents' experiences who live closest to the pain of racial profiling and police misconduct. Otherwise, outcomes are often harmful, expensive, and erode the public's perception of law enforcement.

Based on the LECC's annual spring report in 2017, not one community complaint submitted was found to be upheld. The LECC created a new process to receive community complaints against law enforcement after the End of Racial Profiling Bill passed in 2015, but with zero complaints being substantiated that year, it means that citizens' complaints remain unresolved. To Brandon, this outcome was unacceptable.

Additionally, Brandon was still being racially profiled, and having the police called on him erroneously by racist White security guards. After all Brandon had given in terms of his free time, insights, and expertise to the LECC, he still felt as though he and his peers were being hunted by law enforcement in one way or another. Depending on where they lived, the intensity may vary but the traumatic impact of racial profiling remained consistent. Certain places have more police agencies operating in the district than others, constituting varying levels of intensity in law enforcement scrutiny and actions in those communities.

One of the LECC's subcommittees was overseeing the police training curriculum. They met at the Department of Public Safety Standards and Training (DPSST). Brandon attended a few of their meetings, and it was clear that there was no one with lived experience of being racially profiled in the room contributing to the curriculum in any meaningful way.

T4T's platform, Police-Community Integrated Training and Education (P-CITE) and the Community Conscious Policing public health response model centers the experiences of people who live closest to the pain of law enforcement violence. As someone with lived, educational, and professional experience being racially profiled, Brandon personally felt more qualified than anyone in the statewide training facility, DPSST, to bring insights, intuition, and innovation to the training curriculum. He had worked to fund civilian oversight of police boards in Oakland, settled lawsuits for police misconduct that resulted in disciplinary actions against the officers involved, and advocated on behalf of diverse communities' civil liberties. This expertise was unique on the LECC and DPSST where the training curriculum for all law enforcement is designed and created.

Brandon decided that embedding what the community wants to see in law enforcement training and backing it up with a policy to enforce it was the only way to create true police reform and accountability. It was concerning that very few leaders in law enforcement understood the intricacies of how current police training models actually contribute to racial profiling, increased liabilities and trauma, along with lowering the public's perception of law enforcement over time.

This was the goal for the first Community Conscious Policing workshop, which occurred during the state of emergency in Ferguson, Missouri, the week of November 17, 2014. Brandon's focus transitioned from police accountability to police training. In this process, Brandon would come to understand that there can be no police accountability without up-to-date law enforcement training embedded with a racial equity lens based on experiential learning backed by a policy to enforce it.

Founding T4T

The culturally based rites of passages that Brandon and his partner initiated serve as historically Black and indigenous barometers that measure the impact of their work. These initiations and rites of passages also inform their expertise by providing them with values that preserve life.

This bedrock can be found in the teachings of Prince Hall Freemasonry, Kappa Alpha Psi Fraternity, Inc., Thich Nhat Hanh of Deer Park Monastery and Prophet Neb Naba of the Dogon of the Earth Center.

In Portland, Oregon, Hun and Brandon founded Training 4 Transformation, LLC, (T4T) in the fall of 2014. T4T is an organization that consists of activists, advocates, educators, conflict transformation specialists, trained facilitators, and bridge builders. T4T's mission is to create opportunities for communities and law enforcement to engage in authentic dialogue.

Note: T4T creates opportunities and asks questions enabling law enforcement and their local communities to discover solutions to their own problems through collaboration. By the end of the workshops, T4T aspires to blur the lines between law enforcement and community so that their bonds can strengthen and grow deeper.

Hun earned a Bachelor of Arts degree in Sociology from the University of California, Santa Barbara (UCSB). Next, she earned a Master of Arts degree in Peacebuilding and Conflict Transformation from the School for International Training (SIT), which provided her with the theory, practice, and skills necessary to address conflict at its core.

As a program associate for the Conflict Transformation Across Cultures (CONTACT) program at SIT, Hun was responsible for supporting peacebuilders from more than 70 countries in undertaking a powerful process of study, self-reflection, and collaborative problem-solving within a multicultural environment. In addition, she guided participants through complex conflict-management situations.

Peacebuilders like Hun know that until one begins to do the work on healing broken or wounded relationships, violence will continue. She is a mindfulness and meditation practitioner who studied under Thich Nhat Hanh, a Zen master and peace activist.

Zen Master Thich Nhat Hanh and his teachings have shaped T4T's work both in subtle and explicit ways. Thich Nhat Hanh, known lovingly to his students as Thay, which means teacher. He founded the Engaged Buddhism movement, where he and his students entered the bombed streets of Vietnam to help victims of the war.

In the summer of 2005, Brandon's wife and co-founder of T4T, Hun Taing, joined the second People of Color Retreat at Deerpark Monastery. Being in the presence of 500 Black, Indigenous, and people of color (BIPOC) mindfulness practitioners was a powerful experience for Hun. For five days, she lived like the monks and nuns, practicing mindful walking, mindful eating, mindful speech, meditating, qigong, and being present. This was the first time she had experienced internal peace.

For example, during a morning meditation, attendees were invited to meditate and send healing, loving energy to East Timor to support the thousands suffering from a devastating earthquake. In that moment of collective silence and meditation, Hun felt energy radiating and coalescing from all the bodies in the room. It felt like her individual energy was merging with the collective, and the physical boundary of her body and the group was blurred.

Hun was fortunate that Thay was present at this retreat. She submitted her intentions to receive the Five Mindfulness Trainings and was given the dharma name of Genuine Awareness of the Heart. The Five Mindfulness Trainings are rooted in the Five Precepts offered by the Buddha. They offer a framework to concretely practice mindfulness through our actions, speech and thinking to transform ourselves and society.

The core of Thay's teaching that permeates T4T's work is the importance of personal transformation. One cannot obtain peace and justice in society until one does the individual work of healing and transformation. We begin to transform society by transforming ourselves. On the contrary, there's an unhealthy pattern in today's diversity, equity, inclusion, and justice work in which organizations focus their resources and energy on fixing the external systems without transforming the internal systems and processes that create inequities. Similarly, in social justice movements, activists expend all their energy on fighting institutions, laws, and practices that are unjust. In the process, oftentimes, they end up replicating the same oppressive process if there isn't time or capacity for them to dedicate on their own internal transformation work. Self-transformation, healing, and liberation is an ongoing journey, but it's one that must be practiced on a daily basis in order to change the world.

The other core teaching of Thay that frames Hun's work is interbeing. The reality that people are interdependent. In other words, what I do affects you and what you do affects me. Thay teaches that there's no independent self. Human beings are all interconnected. Therefore, to support the well-being of our community and environment, we must first discover how to support ourselves. This reality is emphasized in T4T's work with law enforcement. They work to dismantle the separation of law enforcement and impacted communities by facilitating spaces where the two groups can see themselves in one another.

T4T specializes in bringing people together across differences, particularly during critical moments in history. T4T works with police officers and survivors of brutality. The foundation of the work is to create opportunities where community members and police officers can authentically listen, share, learn, and connect through humanizing their respective experiences, thus transforming the interpersonal and intercultural relationships within the community.

T4T started in the beautiful college town of Corvallis, Oregon. Working in partnership with the City of Corvallis Police Department and NAACP's Corvallis/Albany branch, T4T delivered an unprecedented community-building workshop where the police department had the opportunity to engage with local community members in confronting issues of profiling, stereotyping, and prejudice. Workshops like these are how the experiences of community members and law enforcement officers are humanized. Humanize, in this context, means to be able to see the other as a fellow person, not an enemy. In this case, officers came in plain clothes not police uniforms.

For activists and advocates, cultivating relationships with police departments yields many benefits for the community. Chief Jon Sassaman and his leadership team invited Brandon to participate in their oral review board evaluations. These interview evaluations gave him valuable insight into the standards and rigor of their hiring process.

CALEA Accreditation

Nearly all of the candidates T4T recommended were hired and retained through the police academy. Brandon served as a community member on panels that consisted of university officials, senior officers, business and local community representatives, students, and neighbors. Corvallis PD has regularly qualified for the prestigious Commission on Accreditation for Law Enforcement Agencies (CALEA), which is considered to be the gold standard by some in public safety. This means that Corvallis PD tracks more data (including race) than is required for CALEA per officer, per stop, etc. Brandon was able to administer a student survey confirming biased policing, which proved to be in alignment with the community's lived experience than CPD's statistics.

CALEA accreditation is absolutely recommended as a necessary action that all non-accredited law enforcement organizations should take immediately, even for small or rural PD's that have limited staff and budget. Remember to always choose preserving life over budget or staffing concerns. Communities should tell city councils, town administrators, or budget directors to move the money from something else that doesn't preserve life.

However, CALEA accreditation falls egregiously short in one specific area, civilian complaints. Current CALEA standards erroneously dictate a complaint process managed and conducted by law enforcement personnel, this is incorrect. CALEA standards on complaints about officers should state the necessary implementation of independent fully funded community oversight of law enforcement boards with the power to hire and fire the police chief or commissioner akin to the previously mentioned CPRB in Oakland.

T4T's success in Corvallis led to an opportunity to host a second community building workshop; this time it was on the state level. T4T was asked to participate in the FBI National Academy of Associates Oregon Chapter (not affiliated with the Federal Bureau of Investigation) statewide training in Oregon.

Approximately 100 chiefs, sheriffs, captains, and lieutenants from across the state of Oregon attended the Community Conscious Policing training that was hosted by the FBI National Academy of Associates, along with 60 diverse community members.

This was the annual meeting, which occurred during the state of emergency in Baltimore the week of April 27, 2015, for police leadership for all departments in the state.

The five things that made this event unprecedented was it was the first time there was BIPOC-led training in the DPSST; it was the first time a community-led training had ever occurred (previously it was always law enforcement training law enforcement); and law enforcement participated without uniforms and guns.

The consensus from all participants was that community members and local police needed more facilitated opportunities to interact, learn, listen, share, and build with one another. Those who were policing well understood that community engagement and cultivating trust are the foundation to creating public safety.

The *Columbian* newspaper in Vancouver, Washington, featured T4T's Diversity Team. It quoted Brandon saying, "Rather than trying to eliminate all bias in law enforcement, T4T is working to encourage departments to develop compassion and respect for the various demographics living in officers' respective jurisdictions (Gillespie, 2015)."

In the article, the *Columbian* detailed Klamath Falls Police Department Chief David Henslee's thoughts on the program:

> "I was pleased with the open engagement and personal interaction between law enforcement and community members," he said. "The training provided an opportunity for participants to have honest and meaningful dialogue about issues that impact human interactions."

The transformation of relationships, organizations, and society requires a deep commitment to justice, healing, and community building. It's emotionally challenging, time-consuming, and not a one-size-fits-all model. Transformation requires authentic opportunities to engage, listen, share, and be heard.

The work that T4T does and the timing in which they accomplished it is truly unique. They have spent countless hours over the last two decades researching and understanding law enforcement agencies and their responses to police killings, police misconduct, and racial profiling. Furthermore, T4T has dug deep to retain curriculum, trainers, modules, and consultants police have hired to improve upon their practices.

However, there are still components missing. Funding for law enforcement and community members must be allocated in order to build trust and transform relationships in a safe environment with highly skilled facilitators. Law enforcement agencies must begin tracking excessive-force incidents and making all data collected related to vehicles, bicyclists, and pedestrian stops public. The Newark Police Department publishes transparency data on its website in a manner readily accessible to the public. Their 2021 data is not flattering—it clearly shows a practice of discriminatory policing without accountability, which is why it appears accurate (NPD Transparency Data, 2021).

Law enforcement must partner with educational institutions and learn from grassroots, community-led organizations related to social justice and transformative learning. Lastly, community oversight of police and accountability boards—such as the National Association for Civilian Oversight of Law Enforcement (NACOLE)—must be established *and* funded, everywhere law enforcement agencies and activities exist.

Chapter 12

What's Missing in Police Accountability and Criminal Justice Reform?

Proposed plans for police accountability generally focus on several key areas. Most are simply outdated. They are one-size-fits-all and that's why many of them do not make a lasting impact. They're useful for checking boxes, but not for cultural and spiritual paradigm shifts.

Community Conscious Policing means communities would have power over their police departments, including hiring, promotion, termination, tactics, discipline, and training of police chiefs and their subordinates. **Measures that don't include a shift of power are a part of the problem.**

Implicit bias plans rely on training rooted in Harvard University's implicit bias doctrine (Lopez, 2017). Implicit bias is one's subconscious attitude about race, compiled of past perceptions and emotional experiences (or lack thereof), that form a premature judgement of people before proper investigation has occurred. I discussed this when Janice Gassam Asare interviewed me for *Forbes* in 2018, in an article titled "Diversity Trainings Usually Fail."

The implicit association test from Harvard University is at the core of many of these implicit-bias trainings that police departments use. The implicit association test is supposed to determine a person's subconscious racism. Training based on this test was ineffective at reducing incidents of excessive use of force or police misconduct (Kaste, 2020).

It seems as though there's a disconnect between the intended use and the public's perception of these tests. The perception is that there is a causal link between changes in implicit bias and changes in discriminatory behavior. However, the more you begin to unpack this causal link, the more you realize how weak it actually is.

In "A meta-analysis of change in implicit bias," researchers examined about 500 studies over 20 years involving about 81,000 participants that used the implicit association test and similar measures. Trainings based on the implicit association test do a variety of things such as:

> "...exposing people to pictures of admired Black people and despised White people...
>
> ...exposing people to admired White people and disliked Black people...
>
> ...taking the perspective of a Black person...
>
> ...making anti-prejudiced norms salient prior to measuring implicit bias towards Black people.
>
> ...the threat of confirming a negative stereotype...
>
> ...the threat of giving a speech in front of a panel of judges...
>
> ...holding a multi-digit number in their heads, prior to or during the implicit measure.
>
> ...asking "How warm do you feel toward Black people?"

They concluded that there is very little evidence that changes in implicit bias have anything to do with changes in behavior. To change behavior, one must go further. In a nutshell, implicit bias training doesn't change individual, institutional, or systemwide actions.

NYPD Dodges 2,500 Complaints of Bias

The New York Police Department (NYPD), whose staff had been exposed to implicit bias training, also collected roughly 2,500 complaints regarding implicit bias over a four- or five-year period and neglected to substantiate any of them, according to the Office of the Inspector General (OIG), Department of Investigation (DOI) in 2019.

NYPD ignored complaints unless they "alleged that an officer used a racial slur *and* took additional police action (e.g., making an arrest)" according to NYC DOI in the June 26, 2019, public report entitled "Complaints of Biased Policing in New York City: An Assessment of NYPD's Investigations, Policies, and Training." As of the OIG-NYPD Sixth Annual Report in April 2020, these problems still persist, and complaints of bias policing remain unaddressed.

New York City's primary agency for investigating allegations against police officers, the Civilian Complaint Review Board (CCRB), doesn't investigate complaints of biased policing (Budryk, 2019), defined as "discriminatory policing based on race, ethnicity, color, national origin, creed, disability, sexual orientation, gender identity, gender, age, citizenship status, alienage, housing status, and other non-physical characteristics" (NY DOI, 2019). NYPD does not monitor biased policing allegations made against its uniformed and other employees with the same depth and diligence that NYPD brings to tracking excessive force. The NYPD and the CCRB also neglected to share this information with the City's Commission of Human Rights (CCHR) to aid in investigative efforts into individualized or systemic discrimination against members of the public according the 2019 report. It's clear that attempts at reform have been made, but bias and brutal policing are resilient.

Many people, from the US Department of Justice to individual police departments, talk about community-oriented policing, yet they are not practicing it, and those attempting to are not doing it well enough. Brandon wanted to build upon the current state of community policing in order to create something deeper, more comprehensive, and authentic.

What's missing and needed is transformation, specifically the opportunity to transform community relationships with law enforcement. Training models fail to bring diverse community members, people of color who have experienced biased policing, or survivors of police violence together with officers in any meaningful or productive way. Plans fail to put any power into the hands of survivors. Without this key component, many efforts are in vain as there is no true accountability.

It is not enough to ban chokeholds. Officers must be trained (using reallocated funds) in arrest techniques that don't rely on pain compliance, pulmonary constriction, or respiratory compression.

Pain compliance includes arrest methods that rely on inducing pain through various techniques and equipment to control someone. This isn't possible because pain stimulates the fight or flight response involuntarily. These techniques can end in brutality.

Pulmonary constriction includes arrest techniques that reduce blood flow to the brain and vital organs. Obviously, reducing blood flow to the brain and organs is lethal and can stimulate a person's fight-or-flight response, escalating the situation into another police killing.

Respiratory compression includes arrest techniques that compress or restrict the respiratory system in any way, including holds and methods like tear gas. Stopping a person from breathing is lethal and can also stimulate the fight-or-flight response, escalating the situation into another police killing.

A team of non–law enforcement, non–military martial arts experts versed in nonviolent techniques must be convened to audit and rewrite the police academy curricula in this area. Officers should be required to spend as much time training in these new unarmed techniques as they spend on the training with firearms throughout their career.

Police firearms training is flawed. Officers are trained only to shoot targets at center mass, meaning police officers are only trained to shoot people in the heart or brain: lethal shots. (Jacobo, 2016) Is there any wonder that, if officers spend the majority of their training shooting targets at center mass, police killings are the outcome?!

Police officers are taught that, within a 20-foot radius, a suspect can stab you faster with a knife than you can unholster, aim, and shoot a firearm. Officers then practice shooting center mass more than any other aspect of the job. This is a recipe for police killing that is imposed on officers whether they like it or not. Police firearm training is flawed and should be reformed. Shots other than lethal shots must be practiced for more hours than lethal shots are practiced.

Nearly all diversity trainings are preached to police in a vacuum without providing tools and support needed to engage real people in the neighborhood. Many diversity training for law enforcement are led by White men.

When T4T first began training with the City of Corvallis Police Department, facilitators gained access to their training materials from the Museum of Tolerance in Los Angeles. While serving as a governor-appointed board member for the Law Enforcement Data Collection and Policy Review Committee in the state of Oregon, one of the subcommittees was addressing the training curriculum for the Department of Public Safety Standards and Training, where all of law enforcement are trained in the state. Their manual at that time was named, "Diversity and Profiling in Contemporary Policing (Tactical Ethics II)." It was considered to be a follow-up training to the Museum of Tolerance's Perspectives on Profiling curriculum that T4T had critiqued from a racial-equity, communal perspective in Corvallis a few years prior.

It came with a video of scenarios of community members and various police stops or calls that cadets in the academy had to navigate successfully. These courses may have been okay as introductory level courses in the police academy. They do not, however, equip law enforcement officers with the knowledge, awareness, skills, and attitudes necessary to navigate critical spaces where systemic power dynamics and race intersect on a daily basis.

Our Community Conscious Policing model is the next step from scenario-based training. T4T uses live engagement with diverse impacted communities to discover blind spots that may still be hidden beneath the surface. Usually these blind spots show up as racism or ill-perceived dominance; however, they usually stem from a core of trauma. For this reason, accountability is often the first step toward healing.

Another red flag regarding training was that the trainers or curriculum designers were often police officers who were previously disciplined for actions, such as policy violations or actually breaking the law. While Brandon served on the LECC, the Civil Rights Director for the Oregon Department of Justice allegedly was being racially profiled by his own colleagues. What made this ironic was that the ODOJ was charged by the governor to establish the LECC as a result of the End of Racial Profiling Bill in 2015.

How can the office charged with ending racial profiling actively participate in the racial profiling of its own civil rights director?

Oregon Civil Rights Director

Mr. Erious Johnson, Civil Rights Director at the Oregon Department of Justice, filed suit in 2016 after it came to light that he had been the subject of "digital stakeout" (digital surveillance operation) by one of his own colleagues at the DOJ. Johnson was allegedly racially profiled by his own colleagues while working for the Attorney General's Office (Dorn, 2017).

Carolyn Walker at the Portland law firm Stoel Rives prepared the DOJ report at the request of the Attorney General (AG). The AG wanted "an independent and critical" look into why DOJ investigators were looking at Oregonians using the "Black Lives Matter" hashtag on social media. Walker found that "intelligence unit employees had not received adequate cultural competency training, or training on anti-racial profiling, hidden or implicit bias, and/or diversity training."

The reason why this is significant is because the same people who were given a budget paid for by tax dollars to set up processes to end racial profiling in law enforcement for the state, were themselves being sued for racially profiling their only Black male director, who happened to lead their Civil Rights work. This is an example of why Brandon felt motivated to design better processes from the ground up with the guidance of people who lived, worked and sacrificed for a safer community. The goal of Community Conscious Policing is to support each neighborhood and city to reimagine what public safety should look like in the 21st century.

The LECC office overseeing law enforcement training for the state of Oregon from 2006–2016 was doing so during a very polarized time with Black Lives Matter community uprisings nationwide.

Police Captain's Scandal

Captain Sam Kamkar was "accused of photographing his subordinate's cleavage and put on leave." His cases then became unprosecutable as a result. Every police officer, sheriff, and private security officer in the state goes through certification at DPSST where Kamkar led training around implicit bias. Kamkar was in charge of curriculum design for the Department of Public Safety Standards and Training (DPSST) in Salem between 2006 and 2017.

Sam Kamkar is why Brandon didn't include Eugene PD in his book initially, although their CAHOOTS program is gaining national acclaim for providing mental health support in response to 911 calls instead of police (Andrew, 2020). All praise is due to those officers and community members who are setting a precedent for others to learn from. Other cities, such as Oakland, are adopting the CAHOOTS model as a public health response to ending law enforcement violence against community members who have historically been most impacted by police while experiencing a mental health crisis.

There seems to be a correlation between law enforcement trainers, previous controversial cases related to racial profiling or crimes against women, and being hired or promoted to train the next generation of law enforcement. This was a cycle that Brandon witnessed.

On April 18, 2018, Brandon was hired by the City of Portland to establish the new Committee on Community-Engaged Policing. This was part of the Portland Police Bureau's compliance with the federal U.S. Department of Justice settlement agreement from January 10, 2014. One of the goals was to improve the police bureau's relationship with communities of color.

Below is a message that Brandon wrote to the U.S. Department of Justice, who was overseeing the Portland Committee on Community Engaged Policing to ensure that it met the final stipulation of the settlement agreement between the DOJ and the City of Portland Police Bureau, who found in 2012 that the police had used excessive force against people experiencing a mental health crises. They didn't focus on race, which was a problem. Attached are Brandon's recommendations, some of which were ignored.

The date of the final report was December 14, 2018.

Final Report on Portland Committee on Community Engaged Policing (PCCEP) Continuing Education.

Below are themes that should be included in PCCEP Continuing Education to ensure its success. Without them, the committee may not be prepared for upcoming challenges. All of these topics, and more, can be found in our educational resource *Best Practices in Community Conscious Policing: A Reflection on Law Enforcement Community Building Workshops* (2nd edition). I highly recommend that each committee member be provided with a copy to support them in their respective roles on PCCEP. I will offer them at no charge.

The book consists of relevant legislation, violence reduction models, best practices from mental health law enforcement programs nationwide, community oversight board references, and a historical perspective on law enforcement community relations here in Portland, Oregon. What makes it unique is that I am one of the few, if not only, community members who bring lived experience from actually settling a lawsuit against a police department and participating in helping to successfully fund a community oversight board. Additionally, T4T's experience leading local branches of the NAACP, ACLU and SEIU are always invaluable.

The following is a Summary of Themes for PCCEP Continuing Education.

1. The **City of Portland's Racial Equity understanding is** currently nonexistent and is a concern for potential liabilities and trauma.

2. Portland should follow **Models of Community Oversight Boards** currently existing in the U.S. City of Portland community oversight of law enforcement boards need to have subpoena authority, evidentiary hearings, able to amend the City Charter in 2020 to establish discipline authority

3. **Independent Rubric** to measure PCCEP progress from established organizations like the National Association of Civilian Oversight of Law Enforcement (NACOLE)

4. **Models/References** of successful Mental Health partnerships between law enforcement organizations, public health providers and community

5. **Relevant Legislation,** ex. Measure LL–Oakland 2016

6. **Relevant Training to PPB:**

- Marshall Project (de-escalation)

- Operation Ceasefire—group violence reduction strategies (Oakland, California)

7. Is **'Community Policing'** the best model for rebuilding trust between law enforcement and community?

8. PPB Training Curriculum Oversight:

- Implicit bias & procedural justice

- Feedback: lack of a racial equity lens, compliance focused rather than healing-centered

- PPB lacks trainers of color (mentioned in 2006 Listening session report)

- Who is reviewing PPB stop-data analysis from a community of color/mental health perspective?

9. **Compile and Audit** current services, programs, committees such as PCCEP, CRC and IPR for the general public in one location. Consolidate resources into one effective community oversight board that is modeled after other successful examples in other places. Oakland and Berkeley are two good places to begin.

10. All existing policies, procedures, curriculum, budget allocation, processes, participants, facilitators, and leaders related to PCCEP should be reevaluated using a **Racial Equity Lens**.

- Without T4T present, there are very few staff from the City of Portland who are qualified to offer a consistent racial equity lens to the PCCEP process and committee.

- It is essential that people of color with lived experience in facilitating cultural and systemic paradigm shifts lead members of the dominant culture in this process.

- Educational and professional experience should also be considered, but lived experience is vital.

- By implementing a mental health response, without first implementing a racial equity lens, the PCCEP will simply be doing "business as usual" and be susceptible to making no substantive change to meet the community's needs.

The 100 days of protest was a year later. Not to mention the fact that Portland hired Danielle Outlaw as the first African American woman police chief in the department's history. She was the director of internal affairs in the Oakland Police Department who had upheld the officers who had detained Brandon in front of his grandmother's home where he had grown up the day before attending graduate school. Brandon knew based on how protestors were mistreated by the Oakland Police Department during the international Occupy Movement that Chief Outlaw was going to ultimately support the police through any misconduct allegations made by community members, protestors and residents. Outlaw had similar difficulties in Philadelphia, where she serves as a Police Commissioner. She ended up laying the groundwork, in Brandon's opinion, for the 100 days of protest in Portland shortly after she left. And Portland hired her to be the police chief! They ignored people like him who provided feedback, like the first editions of this book, and Portland ended up embarrassing itself on national TV when the mayor, who Brandon used to advise through PCCEP, got maced by law enforcement on national news and feuded with former President Donald Trump. At the core of the issue, Trump had sent national troops into Portland to end the protests, because in his opinion, Mayor Wheeler had lost control of nightly community uprisings downtown.

Brandon and his partner thought that it was time for community members who lived closest to the pain of racial profiling and police misconduct to bring their insights and intuition to the forefront in a brave space designed for them where innovative ideas could manifest without the pressure of staring at a badge, police uniform or gun triggering memories that are traumatizing. Police, researchers and lawyers couldn't reimagine public safety without being led by people who experience it daily.

Chapter 13

T4T Explained

T4T is a certified minority business enterprise (MBE/ESB) that works with government, private, civic, and nonprofit sectors to create a culture of diversity, equity, inclusion, and justice.

T4T trainers are multilingual, experts in curriculum development and instructional design, and certified in conflict transformation. They have lived experience abroad while maintaining local roots. (It's a prerequisite for the trainers to have international experience. This includes living in another country in addition to the U.S., speaking a language in addition to English, holding a master's degree in their professed area of expertise, and a verified good reputation.)

T4T integrates models and resources from global peacebuilding movements into local situations. Depending on the needs of each client, T4T offers a range of services that help organizations to make cultural shifts. They bring a demonstrated commitment to race equity and incorporate structural power analysis into the work, with knowledge and understanding of how power manifests in matters of race, ethnicity, age, sexual orientation, gender identity and expression, religion, physical ability, and socio-economic circumstances.

Their workshops have transcended traditional barriers, such as police officers being shut down, community members being re-traumatized or triggered, and processes being corrupted in some way by political influence.

T4T's focus is on shifting law enforcement's approach to problem solving, including, but not limited to: integrating conscious leadership principles based on emotional intelligence and seen with a racial equity perspective, healing-centered approaches, culturally responsive training, and de-escalation strategies. Experiential learning is the model, pioneered by Brandon and Hun's alma mater, the School for International Training Graduate Institute.

T4T applies the 77 Commandments and the tenets of Kemetic spirituality to provide a standard to judge their actions and evaluate the ideas of others as they work to correct the system. This makes them accountable to some of the oldest Black people on Earth, the Dagomba (Dogon) of Ouagadougo, Burkina Faso. It also makes T4T able to constantly identify errors in individual and systemic behaviors that create injustice when racist, unjust institutional cultures seek to adapt in the face of accountability in an effort to preserve their destructive behaviors.

T4T strives to preserve life first, above optics, liability, and the owners' agendas. There is a way to harmonize the dialogue of energies in those involved so that law enforcement officers, suspects, and all people can live long healthy lives. This is what distinguishes T4T from many other diversity training that relies on the same implicit association test to frame their work.

T4T designs spaces that focus on live engagement and the power of reflection on lived experiences. All participants can be brave, vulnerable, and critical yet compassionate. Colleagues and community are able to confront biases, rebuild a shared vision of community, and connect in ways that otherwise may never have happened.

More importantly, what has emerged is an innovative co-creative process that T4T has trademarked Community Conscious Policing. This curriculum was developed with the participation of the City of Corvallis Police Department, FBI National Academy Association, and hundreds of community members.

The T4T Approach

T4T confronts bias, prejudice, discrimination, privilege, and oppression through a co-creative experiential learning process. The answers community and law enforcement seek for reducing police killings can be found in a transparent and co-creative structure that empowers all members of the area to provide solutions to the prevalent issues in a specific community. The transparent and co-creative structure refers to T4T working to receive input from all stakeholders, including law enforcement, prioritizing people who live closest to the pain and those impacted the most.

It's important that efforts today are in alignment with movements that preceded them like the Public Health Response Model to end law enforcement violence from the Black Panthers, and that proper respect is given to the ancestors and elders who paved the way. Additionally, rather than creating new groups, it is important to support the organizations who led the way in dismantling barriers to access for not only Black people, but for everyone else who built their legacy upon the foundation they established in this country. For this reason, T4T incorporates lessons that have been passed mouth-to-ear for generations.

T4T invites law enforcement to reach out to members of the general population, being careful not to focus solely on community, political, and religious leaders. When T4T worked with the Corvallis Police Department, many police officers were concerned that this workshop could be interrupted or cancelled by Black Lives Matter protesters, like so many other City Council meetings during that time in Portland. Luckily, both Hun and Brandon were involved in diverse communities around town, which made it easy to be in partnership with the friends who expressed their First Amendment rights through protest. All other efforts to sabotage progress were red herrings to keep the focus from accountability and healing.

T4T did not, and doesn't need to, advertise on social media to recruit community members to participate in Community Conscious Policing workshops. Social media isn't recommended because it doesn't require fact-checking, which makes it an environment that generates misinformation. This makes outreach efforts more difficult. However, T4T spread the outreach portion of the process over three months in order to meet people where they are in the community and invite them to participate.

Regarding outreach efforts, in some cases Brandon and Hun volunteered serving meals or giving away clothes for a period of time before earning the respect of community members. As community members trusted Brandon and Hun, they were introduced to others and given the opportunity to be a resource and contribute to the wellbeing of other families. This process took time.

Hun is a descendant of Dolores Huerta's lineage of labor union organizing. The model "each one teach one" is found in the Black Panther's and Huerta's philosophies. T4T reached out to see what issues were pressing for community members, saw what they needed, and helped them fulfill those needs, before inviting them to participate.

Our outreach strategy includes: communities in recovery; youth; LGBTQA+; Latino/a/x people; Black, Indigenous, and people of color; English language learners; people living with disabilities; people in need of mental health support; immigrants; refugees; people from rural communities; and survivors of domestic violence and abuse. Resist the tendency to exotify (assign an exciting meaning) this list and include diverse people who live in the impacted jurisdiction.

These are people T4T sought for inclusion in dialogue or process, so that they could be heard directly by decision makers. T4T strives for inclusivity by inviting diverse groups in during outreach. Readers should do searches for organizations in their area and contact them via those websites or phone numbers directly.

Often, Brandon volunteered in support of the causes that mattered most to diverse neighbors first. In exchange, they could learn more about Brandon and T4T's work and opportunities to engage directly with local law enforcement in their area.

One of the most powerful memories that Brandon has is when he was able to confront the officers who had forced him out of his own home with an attorney at the community-led Police Review Commission (PRC) hearing in Berkeley, California. Across from Brandon was the Black officer who was the primary perpetrator, and he sat next to the Asian cop who initially had been willing to hear Brandon out during the police stop (however, he did not intervene on Brandon's behalf when the other officers overstepped their bounds by kicking him out of his own home).

The Asian officer shed some tears during the hearing, which demonstrated that he felt remorse for what had happened to Brandon. The Black cop was the worst. He was visibly angry, and Brandon got the chance to simply look him directly in the eyes while his attorney did all of the talking.

At this point, it is important to note Commandment 19, "Thou shall not get angry or enter a dispute without just cause," and Commandment 68, "Thou shall not get angry." In the case of police officers, it seems obvious that anger would result in misconduct, brutality, and killings. Officers should manage their anger. Anger in officers should signal to their superiors that there is a risk for misconduct, brutality, and police killing. Anger is the indicator warning light.

The officer couldn't take the pressure when the PRC asked him questions, and he rudely got up to leave early when it was Brandon's time to testify. The police representative apologized to Brandon on the record for this behavior. Brandon's response, for the record, was that the truth stands. Liars run. The officer acted tough when he kicked Brandon out of his house illegally but displayed insolence in front of the community members who were empowered to render their verdict against him, violating Commandment 51, "Thou shall not act with insolence." Officers who leave their own disciplinary meetings in this manner should be considered in egregious violation of their code of conduct, immediately terminated from employment from law enforcement, have their Police Academy certification revoked, and be barred from further employment in this profession nationally via a yet-to-be created US National Do Not Hire List for law enforcement.

He had no regard for the law or Brandon as a human being. It demonstrated to Brandon that even Black police officers are able to racially profile and uphold racist systems. Before the outcome of his case, one officer died of natural causes. The Asian cop would never be promoted and the Black cop, who was the main aggressor, lost his job. (He had infractions on his personnel file before Brandon's complaint.) This is where Brandon learned that community police accountability boards need access to the files of law enforcement personnel who are accused of racial profiling to see if there is a pattern or practice of similar misconduct. He also learned that it was important to study the policies that govern police behavior while engaging in the community. The changes that he wanted to see in policing had to be embedded in the training and enforced with a policy. Otherwise, there could be no police accountability or reform.

Brandon also discovered that it costs more to sue the police than one usually makes if the case is successful. And that the burden of proof related to racial profiling is virtually impossible to prove in court. It's important to recognize the PRC who decided in Brandon's favor. Their verdict led to a monetary settlement from the police department and disciplinary actions against the officers involved. The path to Brandon's healing also began as a result of their verdict. Brandon was able to transform his energy from accountability into healing from the trauma of police brutality. And he could help others to do the same.

Without accountability, it is nearly impossible to experience deep healing. For this reason, T4T felt it was vital that their neighbors and local police department get an opportunity to engage beyond the typical traffic stop in a space designated for racial justice. "Racial equity work is also about changing systems and centering the experiences and voices of people and communities of color" wrote to Erin Okuno and Heidi Schillinger on March 16, 2017, in their article "Color Brave Space–How To Run a Better Equity Focused Meeting," published on the blog Fakequity.

This process of inclusion for recruitment of diverse impacted communities takes a lot longer than social media posts stay up. By the time T4T hosted Community Conscious Policing workshops, Brandon knew almost every community participant on a first-name basis, their stories, and their reasons for attending. Hun was the architect of this civic engagement model based on her experience in labor union organizing.

T4T focuses its outreach efforts on the general population to gain community access and personally invite the constituents who are often excluded from society so that their voices can be integrated into the process. Its focus is to support accredited law enforcement agencies who are ready for more than module training and are seeking a deeper, more authentic opportunity for community building. T4T also encourages community participants to work with accredited law enforcement agencies, urging them to meet the required standard.

Chapter 14

Case Study #7: Traffic Ticket Dismissed

Brandon was still being followed by police in his car around campus, and even got a red-light ticket dismissed after an officer chose to pull him over instead of the car in front of him that broke the law. Brandon was a lecturer, which means he taught at the University of Delaware but was not tenure track and didn't receive benefits.

When it happened, Brandon was a mile from campus driving in near-blizzard conditions. The streets and sidewalks were empty. He drove to purchase some Jamaican food at a restaurant one mile away from his home. The route he took was simple and involved only one right turn. There was one car ahead of Brandon that he was following. They stopped at the red light and the car ahead of Brandon turned right. Brandon pulled up, stopped, saw the street was clear, and turned right.

As soon as Brandon completed his turn, he was pulled over by law enforcement. Brandon had followed the car ahead of him and didn't understand why he was being pulled over and not the other vehicle.

The officer came to Brandon's vehicle and asked for his driver license and registration. Brandon responded politely. Brandon asked why he was being pulled over, and the officer said, "for turning right at a red light." From the officer's vantage point, he could see both cars, so again Brandon wondered why the other driver wasn't pulled over. Brandon was confused. He asked the officer if there were appeal instructions on the back of the ticket. The officer said, "Yes." To the officer's surprise, Brandon responded, "Ok, I'll see you in court."

There is a learning opportunity here. The officer was all about the outcome, Brandon was most interested in the process. The outcome may be agreed upon, but the manner in which the outcome was decided is where Brandon's concerns needed to be addressed.

Brandon at the time was new to Delaware. Though he had fraternal connections, he didn't go to them for help. For people who are on a budget, there is a service which is prepaid legal services that are essentially like insurance. For 24 hours a day, seven days a week, you'll have access to legal representation. Find out more at https://blee.wearelegalshield.com/.

In Brandon's experience, the service by itself isn't that useful. However, for people like Brandon who use it often enough to begin to understand what questions to ask the attorney, that's when it becomes really useful. If you only use it once a year, you won't even know what to ask, and they will just tell you the law. Luckily, Brandon used LegalShield when he was a legal redress chairman for legal advice on certain cases. Therefore, Brandon had some type of rapport with the department and attorney's office and as a Public Policy major, Brandon had some idea regarding his line of questioning, which is necessary.

Brandon doesn't want to mislead anyone that this is an end-all, be-all service. You have to meet it halfway. Services differ from state to state and Delaware is a small state. So, when Brandon called for his case to let them know he had gotten a ticket, he explained that it was unfair as he had watched the officer let someone go just before he was pulled over.

The attorney didn't confirm or deny anything that Brandon said, but told him "there could be something there we need to look into." The attorney met Brandon for his court date at the courthouse for a traffic hearing.

It was 8:00 am and packing the traffic court was a crowd of only Black and Brown people, who were being serviced by White people only. When Brandon showed up, he was the only one there with an attorney who was an older White gentleman. They went before the judge, who wanted to charge Brandon with a moving violation, fine him, put points on his record, and increase his insurance costs. Brandon asked the judge for a minute to confer with his attorney.

Brandon told his attorney that he was displeased as he could have received the above charges without an attorney present, implying that the attorney wasn't adding any value and had been a waste of money. Brandon could have agreed to this outcome on his own.

This is a good place to pause for a teachable moment. If anyone is stopped by police officers who "just" want to give you a warning or "just" want to "run your information" to make sure they don't have any warrants; the actual goal is to get an individual in the law enforcement system.

It could be a parking ticket at first, which if not paid on time could turn into something else, an increased violation. This becomes a slippery slope. For people who are being targeted by police, especially in cases of racial profiling and biased policing, law enforcement's goal is to get you in their system.

So, Brandon appeals all of his parking tickets and minor violations relentlessly. He defends his credit report, his grades, and anything that has to do with his name on paper with vigor, demanding immediate action. One must be vigilant and defend themselves first.

At the time of the court case for the traffic stop, Brandon just so happened to be applying for doctoral programs. One of the programs he applied to was Teaching English to Speakers of Other Languages (TESOL) at Columbia University. He told his attorney to tell the judge he was preparing to leave Delaware to go to a doctoral program at Columbia University so this was a waste of everyone's time. Brandon had real things to do and didn't need this violation diverting time and resources. After Brandon's lawyer said this to the judge, in front of the officer who issued the ticket, Brandon didn't have his acceptance letter yet, but he had applied, and the judge ruled in Brandon's favor, dismissed the violation, and asked him to pay a small, one-time fee.

Chapter 15

Jonathan's Mentorship

In 2012, after graduate school, Brandon taught at the University of Delaware. While there, he met a gentleman by the name of Jonathan Hall. Brandon was new to the East Coast and visited the Black Cultural Center to meet some of his fraternity brothers since he didn't know anyone. Jonathan recognized that Brandon was new to the BCC, so he introduced himself and offered Brandon something to eat. He only had the honor of knowing Jonathan for maybe 10 months before Brandon accepted a full-time faculty teaching position at Oregon State University.

Shortly after they met, Brandon realized that Jonathan was best friends with one of his fraternity brothers. Often, Jonathan and Brandon would get together with the brothers after work and have lively discussions about police and community relations. This is 2012, right around the time Trayvon Martin was shot and killed by George Zimmerman in Florida. Zimmerman was later acquitted of any wrongdoing, which ignited community uprisings and protests nationwide (Alvarez and Buckley, 2013).

Through lively dialogues with Jonathan, Brandon found out that Jonathan was an education major. He was an educator first, like Brandon. Jonathan graduated from college, became a schoolteacher, and was then inspired to become a school resource officer.

Based on his experience as a teacher, Brandon doesn't believe in law enforcement being in schools. However, he was able to learn first-hand by observing Jonathan how a person could earn respect in the community and in law enforcement without compromising their integrity.

Jonathan was a proud member of Alpha Phi Alpha, the first historically Black intercollegiate Greek-letter fraternity established for Black men (Scott, 2021). He was also a member of a local motorcycle club, a leader of the M.W. Prince Hall Masonic Lodge, and was well respected in the community as a supportive father, husband, uncle, brother, and friend. Jonathan demonstrated compassion, accountability, and leadership in his duties as Lieutenant of the local police department, as well as in the community. One lesson Brandon learned from Jonathan is that every time they would part ways, Jonathan would say, "Text me when you make it home, so I know that you made it safe." Now, Brandon asks Hun, friends, and family to do the same.

Unfortunately, after Brandon left Delaware to take a faculty position at Oregon State University, Jonathan was diagnosed with cancer and passed away shortly thereafter. The first edition of this book was dedicated in memory of him and a percentage of the proceeds were dedicated to the Jonathan Hall Scholarship Fund for his children. Jonathan's nephew Cameron came to live with Brandon and Hun during this time and served proudly as T4T's first college intern.

The last time Brandon and Jonathan spoke, he was forecasting the next time they would hang out and when Brandon would be able to visit again. Jonathan's response was, "Carpe Diem," which means seize the day.

T4T Community Conscious Philosophy

T4T is committed to implementing healing-centered, trauma-informed philosophies and practices into every aspect of their work. Trauma-informed means that services are designed to minimize any possible harm they could produce. Understanding how trauma affects individuals can help to reshape the institutions with trauma-informed systems, which in turn reduces public health costs to the community.

Did you know that emotions have liquid chemical correspondents in the body? They do. This isn't just a statement. Individual and community emotions, empathy, and trauma are discussed throughout this book. It's possible that readers may be vicariously traumatized. Therefore, it is necessary to have a sophisticated understanding of what exactly emotions are in the landscape of police accountability.

What is meant by saying emotions are liquids is that anger's liquid chemical correspondent in the body is cortisol, fear's is adrenaline, worry's is norepinephrine, and joy's is dopamine and serotonin. Dr. Louann Brizendine discusses this in her book *The Male Brain*. These emotions move through your body, internal organs, and brain. When these liquids become out of balance, then you will be emotionally out of balance. It is important to understand that these liquids are running through the nervous systems. Everyone has them.

The first step in healing from trauma is to understand how to manage and balance these liquids internally, interpersonally, and through using trauma-informed systems institutionally. Any sophisticated emotional operation, especially those that help heal from trauma and develop empathy, must include this understanding to be effective.

Efforts by institutions and stakeholders must be trauma-informed and include a deep understanding of human nature. This understanding is embedded into all points of interaction or interface, reducing potential harm to the public.

Chapter 16

Case Study #8: Oregon Security Guard Incident

November 3, 2014, Hillsboro, Oregon

Here is another story of an armed security guard who illegally forced Brandon out of his residential gym at Thorncroft Farm Apartments, Berkshire Communities (TFABC), where he was a renter when he first moved to Oregon. It ended with the security guard being decertified for a year or more, so he couldn't work in security anywhere.

Brandon wrote a letter detailing the incident addressed to TFABC and Arcadia Security and Patrol. In the letter, Brandon states that at 11:36 p.m. on Monday, November 3, 2014, at Thorncroft Farm Apartments located at 2028 NW Thorncroft Drive Hillsboro, OR 97124, Brandon was exercising in his apartment complex's residential gym.

He had his back to the door and headphones on and was interrupted by someone who appeared to be a Hillsboro Police Officer. He was dressed in all black, with what appeared to be a bulletproof vest on his body and what appeared to be a black 9mm or "Glock" firearm in a holster around his waist.

Immediately, the officer ordered Brandon to leave the gym. When Brandon asked the officer why, he told Brandon the gym was closed. The officer made no introduction, so for Brandon's own safety, he had to assume that the officer indeed was a Hillsboro Police Officer.

In light of recent events nationwide where unarmed men of color have been murdered by law enforcement officers, this situation was extremely stress-inducing for Brandon. The officer should have never entered the gym at all!

Brandon asked the officer when the gym closed. He said 10 p.m. Brandon then asked, "When did the closing time for the gym change?" The officer said that it was a recent decision made by the management of the apartment complex and that communication would be made public soon.

As Brandon got his jacket off the floor and began to exit, on the door was a sign that clearly stated the gym was open 24 hours a day. In other words, the gym *never* closes. Being a busy father of two, this is one of the reasons why Brandon chose to live there, because he needs to access a gym any hour of the day. Brandon has a medical condition that requires him to exercise daily and because of his busy schedule, early nights and mornings are the only times for him to work out.

When Brandon showed the officer the sign that read, "OPEN 24 HOURS," he said that the new policy closing access to the gym at 10 p.m. had already taken effect. As a resident, Brandon received *no* notice of this new policy, and told the officer that there should be a sign to indicate this change in schedule.

Brandon's next question was, "Is the gym now closed every day at 10 p.m. or just on certain days?" He also explained that he had developed a routine of working out around 11 p.m. after his family went to sleep, and this new schedule would inhibit his ability to exercise. The officer responded that the gym was closed indefinitely at 10 p.m., and he made it clear that he was speaking on behalf of the property management company of the apartment complex.

As Brandon exited the gym with its sign that read, "OPEN 24 HOURS," the officer said the key code for entry should already be changed to prevent access after 10 p.m. Immediately, Brandon entered the code to both external entry gates and gained access in front of the officer. Then again, Brandon repeated his complaints to the officer.

The officer's reply was, "Management empowered me to enforce this new rule." He offered no other names or specific information. Brandon then asked the officer what time the gym opened, and the officer had to turn his patrol SUV on to find out. The officer told Brandon the gym opened at 8 a.m., and Brandon also asked him to confirm that property management from the apartment complex had indeed implemented this policy. The security guard confirmed this and said that if Brandon had a problem, he should address his concerns with the property manager.

Standing outside in the rain and cold with the officer around midnight, Brandon was embarrassed. Anyone watching them under the streetlight could easily have assumed that Brandon had done something wrong or illegal the way the officer kicked him off the premises. Before Brandon left, he introduced himself to the officer and shook his hand. Brandon asked him for his name, and he replied "Roger." On his vest, it read "CROSS" in big letters. Considering this evidence, he inferred that the security officer's complete name was Roger Cross. After Brandon was ordered to leave, he went home.

At 5:35 a.m. Tuesday morning, a few hours later, Brandon woke up early before his family and returned to the gym to finish his workout. This time, there was no interruption. Exercising is essential for Brandon to maintain good health and balance. He should not have had to explain this to anyone, especially since he didn't violate any existing policy. For this reason, Officer Roger Cross' actions not only triggered memories of past incidents with law enforcement, but also disrupted Brandon's exercise plan. As a result, the officer created a hostile living environment for Brandon and his family.

On Tuesday, November 4, at 9:01 a.m., Brandon met with TFABC's sales consultant, Dani, at the front office of the apartment complex. Brandon shared his story with her and outlined his credentials, observations, and recommendations. Brandon's first question was, "What time does the fitness room/gym close?" Her reply was that it was open 24 hours a day. At that point, Brandon asked for them to sit down so he could provide Dani with details of what happened the previous night.

Dani assured Brandon that the officer was a security officer who worked for Arcadia Security and Patrol, but he was not an actual police officer. Dani assured Brandon that she had received no communication from the property manager regarding a new 10 p.m. closing time in the gym. She then asked

Brandon if it was possible that the security guard was new and confused regarding protocols or procedure. However, Brandon replied that he specifically asked Roger how long he had patrolled the area. Roger said that he had patrolled that district for years. Therefore, Roger made it abundantly clear that he had every authorization to force Brandon out of the fitness area.

Brandon told Dani that it was the apartment complex's obligation, in addition to the security company, to make him whole as a victim, or survivor, of what he observed to be racial profiling. At the very least, it was a confirmed "misuse of authority." Brandon, after this incident, feared for his safety, especially after dark. It could have easily escalated into violence. Roger Cross and Arcadia Security and Patrol knew where Brandon lived and when to find him.

Brandon demanded that Roger Cross not be allowed to perform patrol or security officer duties again. Brandon suggested that Roger be terminated to avoid any future liabilities for Arcadia Security and Patrol or TFBA and that they should invest in some cultural competency training and review existing protocols to ensure residents are not negatively impacted in this way again. After interacting with Arcadia Security officers, the Director of Client Services and the owner, it was clear that there was an organizing principle of intimidation and entitlement.

To this day, no one from Arcadia Security and Patrol has acknowledged this injustice or offered a decent apology. Brandon's grandparents, father, uncles, cousins, and friends have been victims/survivors of this type of misuse of authority. Brandon wishes to ensure this will not continue at the expense of their children.

What Brandon experienced felt like a classic "matter out of place": "anything that looks different looks suspicious and leads to the bias that Black people don't live here, so this person in front of me is suspicious and gives me probable cause to stop them." A rookie mistake because *no crimes have been committed*. Roger Cross, a veteran patrolling this area, should have had proper training to not fall into these assessment or evaluation pitfalls. Seeing a man of color exercising in the gym at 11 p.m. may not have been an image he had seen too often around Hillsboro, Oregon. Since Brandon's family was new, maybe Roger thought Brandon looked "suspicious." Rogers' actions clearly communicated that he was securing the premises from Brandon as a potential threat or intruder, and not securing it for Brandon as a paying resident of this community. Brandon was made to feel like a criminal and, outside of the complex, other neighbors very easily could have made the same assumption. The security officer should never have entered the gym at all.

After cross-referencing what officer Roger Cross had told him with Thorncroft Farm Apartments the following morning, Brandon spoke with Sam Hasson, Director of Client Relations at Arcadia Security.

When Brandon shared who he was and why he was calling, Sam offered no response other than to forward Brandon to legal services. Brandon told Sam that Brandon didn't need a referral, and this would be his final attempt at an amicable resolution.

Sam then asked for Brandon's last name, and he declined to give it to him. Brandon had already been intimidated by one of their officers and feared retaliation. Brandon asked Sam for his name and he declined to give it to Brandon. Brandon said he would follow up with a written formal complaint to Arcadia's headquarters, along with Thorncroft Farm Apartments' property manager and owner. This should have been the end of the story.

A few minutes after Brandon hung up the phone, he got a call from Don, the owner of the security company. Brandon did not give anyone his contact information or authorization for it to be shared, so he found it strange that Don called on Brandon's private line from a phone that was unlisted with a blocked ID. This should never have happened, unless Brandon had given authorization to be contacted. Brandon's personal phone number is not public.

Brandon answered the phone and Don introduced himself as the owner of Arcadia Security. Brandon asked if Don was an attorney. He said no. Don asked what had happened and Brandon said that he was a survivor of what he believe to be a biased incident, specifically racial profiling. Next, Brandon began to share his story and Don interrupted to ask for Brandon's surname and to confirm where he worked.

Brandon replied that he did not feel comfortable disclosing details about his identity as he had felt nothing but intimidation from each employee he had encountered at Arcadia so far. First the officer, Roger, then the director of client services Sam Hasson, and now the owner, Don. All three men demonstrated a lack of sensitivity to what Brandon had endured while at his home, doing nothing wrong. None of them apologized or said anything regarding redressing this injustice. As a result, Brandon ended this discussion with Don. In addition, Don was informed that representatives would be in touch with him on Brandon's behalf.

Brandon had no confidence that what occurred to him would be taken seriously by Arcadia and he certainly didn't feel safer with them on patrol. Until they were removed, he monitored them to ensure his family was protected against bullying or retaliation.

At this point, Brandon wanted several things from Thorncroft Farm Apartments.

First, Brandon wanted to file a restraining order against the security officer for intimidation and misuse of authority. Brandon believed that he had been racially profiled or, at the very least, Roger Cross had demonstrated poor judgement that could have cost lives had it not been for Brandon navigating the situation peacefully. For Brandon's family's sake, he needed to ensure that Roger never returned to the property. For liability's sake, TFBA and Arcadia needed to ensure the family's safety and make them whole again. Brandon highly recommended training in the areas of cultural proficiency, cultural humility, community building, and standard operating procedures when engaging with a diverse community.

Second, Brandon wanted Thorncroft to end professional ties with Arcadia. After speaking with upper management and the owner directly, all of them needed training if they wished to engage successfully with diverse clients and constituents. Brandon recommended Knight Vision Security, which is the preferred vendor of NAACP Oregon and the City of Corvallis. They have experience patrolling and protecting communities, while maintaining positive relationships with neighbors.

They have operations in multiple states, including New York, and cities like Eugene, Oregon. Most importantly, they sponsor and participate in community building workshops with local police agencies to build stronger ties with those they protect. This is the 21st century approach to security, based on the data.

Third, Brandon wanted Roger Cross terminated as a security and patrol officer for removing Brandon from the residential gym that he paid for and for creating false pretenses by which to do so. Roger jeopardized Brandon's health by making unlawful decisions while representing himself as a law enforcement official and put Brandon in a traumatic situation that resulted in a lack of sleep, missing work, having nightmares, and raising his blood pressure.

As outlined in *The New Jim Crow* by Michelle Alexander, this type of policing is a form of terrorism. Brandon has a fundamental problem paying rent to a place that hires companies without proper screening, allowing Brandon to be dehumanized and devalued publicly. This negligence put Brandon's family in jeopardy and at risk for future retaliation and/or bullying unless there was a clear disassociation between the building and Arcadia Security.

Fourth, TFBA and owner(s) needed to be held liable for employing security officers who speak erroneously on their behalf regarding policy decisions that impact residents.

Fifth, Brandon needed to be reassured that TFBA is not a hostile environment for him and his family. In addition, he needed to be reassured that its employees have received some training related to cultural competency, class, and racial profiling to ensure that neither he, nor his son, nor any other resident was mistreated while living there.

Sixth, Brandon wanted to be made "whole" from this unfortunate injustice. Before he included any further specifics on what could be done to right this wrong, he would provide time and space for TFBA management to take necessary action and make a sincere effort to keep his business and his family as tenants.

Brandon's motivation was to ensure the protection of himself, tenants like him, and his family in particular. He refused to be bullied at home, especially by agencies employed with his rent dollars for protection services. Brandon asked that Thorncroft support him in righting this blatant injustice. Brandon deserved better.

On Thursday, November 27, 2014, at 8:01 p.m., Brandon emailed the president and vice president of the NAACP Corvallis Branch to propose a new case.

Brandon proposed the new complaint be the misuse of authority and violation of Brandon's "public accommodation" based on race by an armed residential security guard at his home in Hillsboro. Brandon was unlawfully forced to leave his residential gym after the armed security guard fabricated a policy that he said had been communicated to him by the property manager. It was all a lie. Brandon felt his life was in danger if he didn't comply. NAACP Corvallis Branch president and vice president accompanied Brandon to a meeting with the property manager.

Brandon requested an official letter of support based on a legal analysis of his complaint. He also requested their recommendation moving forward on the following approaches: first, filing a complaint with relevant state agencies; second, a lawsuit against the security company; third, issuing further complaints to the Department of Standards and Training/Bureau of Labor & Industry; and fourth, suing Arcadia Security and Patrol.

Brandon was told Roger, the armed security guard, did not file an incident report with the property management or his security company. Therefore, the only incident report available from the night in question was Brandon's. Also, on October 13th, the property manager sent a specific message to the security company that the gym where he had been forcefully removed was indeed open 24 hours a day. The security officer should not have entered the premises when Brandon was exercising.

Brandon was told by a legal consultant that he was able to request a restraining order against the security officer through a civil lawsuit, which he was interested in pursuing. The complaint forms Brandon would need to complete if he sued were the "Private Security/Private Investigator (PSPI) Allegation of Violation Form" with the Department of Public Safety Standards and Training and a "Public Accommodations Discrimination Complaint" with the Oregon Bureau of Labor and Industry Civil Rights Division. The moral of the story is that, find out who certifies the security guard/office and if they have an area to complain about that guard, what the complaint process is.

The property manager of Brandon's apartment complex was fired, and the contract between Arcadia and all TFABC apartment complexes was severed. Brandon didn't mean to get the property manager fired, because he had become like a friend over the course of living there. Additionally, the property manager was the one who was initially receptive to Brandon's complaint. Brandon later discovered that the property manager, a White man, was married to a Black woman. In the 21st century, people are all so interconnected, meaning nowadays online technology has broken barriers that kept people separate in previous times. It used to be that people were introduced by race first, but nowadays people meet around shared interests.

This incident reminded Brandon of Thich Nhat Hanh's concept of "interbeing." What impacts one person can impact others around them (Garrison Institute, 2017). Suffering is not separate. The project manager had children who were Black and although Brandon was right to defend his civil rights, he realized then that because of his actions, the project manager's family would be impacted negatively during Christmas.

As a result of this ah-ha moment, Brandon wanted to (re)discover trauma-informed and healing-centered models to support law enforcement, schools, institutions, organizations, and leaders through their personal racial equity journeys and organizations' cultural paradigm shifts. This is where Brandon transitioned from focusing only on police accountability and began including healing from the trauma of police brutality.

Without healing from his trauma of past racial profiling incidents, Brandon simply sought to punish the oppressor. If Brandon was not careful moving forward, his pain could drive him to become the oppressor of others where Brandon sat in a position of privilege or authority.

These letters were addressed to Thorncroft Farm Apartments, Berkshire Communities, and Arcadia Security and Patrol, Inc. Copies of the letters Brandon wrote to seek accountability for this matter were also mailed to the president and vice president of his branch of the NAACP where Brandon had served as Legal Redress Committee Chairman.

Chapter 17

The City of Corvallis Police Department Community Building Workshop

As the Legal Redress Committee Chairman for the NAACP Corvallis/Albany Branch, Brandon received dozens of discrimination complaints and racial profiling cases regarding law enforcement from community members in the Oregon cities of Corvallis, Lebanon, Albany, Salem, and Portland. His role was to work with the affected members to educate, empower, and correct the wrong by helping the two parties communicate with each other.

Generally speaking, students and staff of color at Oregon State University complain of racial profiling around town. Most incidents were not reported because the students and staff feared retaliation; students who did complain about police were often followed or targeted by those police, and international students feared deportation. Student–police relationships were strained and trust was broken when hate crimes occurred on or near campus without any follow-up or accountability by police.

Additionally, there were many women who were victims of violent crimes who never received support from law enforcement. Many times, the connection between racial profiling and crimes against women goes unrecognized. When time and resources are spent erroneously pursuing Black people, two things can happen: crimes against women are not investigated and real criminals remain free. An example of this happened in March 2017, when Florida police told Latina Herring, "Stop calling 911" three hours before she was shot and killed by her boyfriend. In this case, biased policing caused an officer to dismiss Herring's pleas for protection.

Consent decrees tend to result from settlements between the U.S. Department of Justice and local or state law enforcement agencies regarding a "pattern or practice" of violations of the civil rights of people. According to *The New World of Police Accountability*, by Samuel Walker and Carol Archbold (2014):

> "In New Orleans, the consent decree required by the United States Department of Justice against the New Orleans Police Department went a step beyond previous settlement agreements in two meaningful ways:
>
> 1. It included a section on Gender Bias. The report required new police policies related to the investigation of sexual assault cases and the handling of domestic violence incidents.
>
> 2. It included formal requirements designed to ensure greater community input into the implementation of the consent decree and into the police department once the consent decree had been lifted."

According to the Massachusetts Supreme Court in 2016, there are valid reasons for communities of color and people experiencing a mental health crisis to distrust law enforcement (ACLU, 2016).

The Massachusetts Supreme Court, referring to an ACLU report on "Field Interrogation Observations (FIO)" used by the Boston Police, wrote: "Rather, the finding that Black males in Boston are disproportionately and repeatedly targeted for FIO encounters suggests a reason for flight totally unrelated to consciousness of guilt. Such an individual, when approached by the police, might just as easily be motivated by the desire to avoid the recurring indignity of being racially profiled as by the desire to hide criminal activity."

Once NAACP Corvallis Albany/Branch expressed interest in working in partnership with the Corvallis Police Department, Lieutenant Jim Zessin contacted Brandon for a meeting. NAACP Corvallis Albany/Branch administered surveys to members of the African Student Association (ASA) at OSU to see if they had endured experiences and learned about a letter that had been left at the women's center on campus targeting the only Black woman working there. She happened to be African but was also a U.S. citizen. The letter constituted a hate crime.

Brandon was the faculty advisor of the ASA, and therefore felt obligated to offer support to the group as most of them were away from home. Brandon had his fraternal affiliations and his position within the NAACP gave him the opportunity to support these students on campus and in the community.

Most of the ASA anonymous surveys indicated that the students had experienced racism on campus and in the community. Most of them identified with being racially profiled by law enforcement. The only thing that was not mentioned in the surveys was which specific police department had profiled them. Without this information, Brandon couldn't hold anyone accountable for what had happened. However, he remembered from his case study in Oakland that there was a limited amount of time to file a complaint against the officers; and secondly, he remembered that the ACLU had written a letter of support in that case.

Training Lieutenant Jim Zessin arrived at Brandon's office in plain clothes in September 2014. This disarmed Brandon, because he was expecting a "big, bad" cop like the ones who had harassed him growing up in Oakland. They sat down to talk, and he opened up about his experiences as a minority in the Marines. Then, he shared his vision of equity in law enforcement, elaborated on the chief's investment into training and education for his leadership, and the ways in which officers should be held accountable when boundaries were crossed. Lieutenant Zessin took a personal interest in Brandon, inquiring about his childhood and family.

Hun and Brandon met later with Zessin, police union president Sergeant Michael Mann, and police instructor Officer Nick Hurley. Upon arriving at the police department, Jim gave them a thorough tour of the facilities. Zessin showed Hun and Brandon where evidence is stored, how it is checked in, and the checks and balances ensuring its security. They saw where the officers trained, and Jim introduced all the officers and staff on duty. He was transparent on where they hoped to improve and where they had already made great strides.

Their first order of business was to get to know one another. Brandon shared his numerous experiences of being racially profiled by law enforcement in California, Georgia, Delaware, and Texas.

Brandon shared the experience of filing a complaint after being racially profiled at his own home in Berkeley. He talked about the generations of Black men in his family who had been harassed and profiled by law enforcement. He spoke about its impact on himself and his family. The Corvallis officers shared their experiences with diversity, the challenges of being a police officer, what they enjoyed most about their jobs, and their inspiration for becoming police officers. It was the first time Hun and Brandon got to know officers beyond their badges.

For example, one officer grew up in rural Oregon and had never met a Black person until he went to college. He didn't grow up racist; rather, he simply hadn't met anyone who looked or lived differently until he left home. It didn't diminish his enthusiasm to embed equity in policy, staff, and budgetary decisions. In fact, he went out of his way to value diversity, and supported the collaboration wholeheartedly.

CPD and T4T wanted to recreate the experience of validation and humanization that Brandon personally did not believe was possible before. CPD and T4T were determined to recreate this opportunity for others with the goal of, in Lt. Zessin's words, "humanizing our respective experiences" and to bring people together who might otherwise remain at a perpetual distance.

The Process

Brandon's first impression of the CPD leadership was that they were extremely educated, not only about police tactics, but also about 21st century leadership practices centered on empathy, compassion, and emotional intelligence.

During the Jim Crow era of segregation and even slavery, officers simply escalated one level beyond a suspect to maintain control of a situation. This means that officers made sure to maintain tactical superiority over suspects, including superior firearms, superior numbers, superior vehicles, superior surveillance, etc. That is nearly always counterproductive.

T4T's 21st century conscious leadership supports leaders of organizations in shifting their approach to problem solving. Their first step as a team was to learn more about CPD and how they trained their officers around inclusion. They admitted that their agency was made up of mostly White men. They still wanted the input, however, on recruiting, retaining, and training through a community lens.

Second, T4T evaluated their Museum of Tolerance Diversity Training Manual. For weeks, Hun and Brandon reviewed the manuals, videos, and training resources that CPD provided in good faith. The couple kept the contents of these materials confidential. Their biggest criticism was that the curriculum relied too much on outdated simulated scenarios versus real-life community engagement. It didn't require officers to purge themselves of racism or unconscious bias.

When training is driven by public perception, police leaders wrongly assume that new knowledge will change officer behavior and positively impact the public's perception of the police. Renee J. Mitchell and Lois James found that "training effects will never be truly understood without evaluating a training program to see if it (1) creates positive behavioral change in police and (2) if those behavioral changes improve the public's perception of police" (Mitchell/James, 2018).

For example, the curriculum promoted virtues like color blindness, service, protection, and security, which are necessary to be effective while on duty, but it did not give officers the tools to confront internalized bias, privilege, and oppression. The training video regarding excessive force used dash cam footage from patrol cars that was decades old.

In addition, officers were trained for worst-case scenarios in nearly every engagement with the community. Their lives are at stake, but the safety and civil rights of community members is just as important to protect.

By the time T4T delivered the feedback to CPD, the nation had erupted into a polarized dialogue over Michael Brown, an unarmed Black teen that was killed by police in Ferguson, Missouri. There were community uprisings nationwide as the country waited to hear if Officer Darrin Wilson would be charged.

As tensions among the students at Oregon State University rose, Hun and Brandon decided they needed to do something. With his teacher trainer experience and her expertise in conflict transformation, they researched additional police training methods. When T4T encountered officers who were involved in shootings, the officers said they were simply following training protocol. The U.S. DOJ sometimes mandates training and accountability measures through consent decrees and settlement agreements to help departments, like Ferguson's police department, to implement reform. Hun and Brandon discovered that no training was available where law enforcement could engage directly with the community they served through a professionally facilitated, equity-focused dialogue.

As a former English as a Second Language (ESL) collegiate faculty member, Brandon was reminded of an increasing number of international students and refugees who would engage with local police for a variety of reasons. At Portland Community College, he saw firsthand how campus police received little to no training on how to engage with minority demographics of students such as transgender, formerly incarcerated, undocumented, and international students.

First, public safety officers were not required to maintain the same type of training that campus administrators did in regard to diversity, equity, and inclusion. They were exempt from any type of continuing education in equity. They often did not understand how their uniforms could trigger emotional trauma in students who had negative interactions with law enforcement. They did not understand how students who were formerly incarcerated and working to rebuild their lives, or transgender students who could have the police called on them for using the "wrong" bathroom, could be intimidated by their presence.

Female students received little to no support from the campus police after they reported incidents of stalking or harassment. Black, Latino/a/x, Indigenous, and other students of color also felt that their safe space was taken over by outside authorities any time officers came into the Multicultural Center or if they had to walk past law enforcement parked in their cars on their way to class.

The officers' lack of cultural competence training often translated into some form of trauma for students, faculty, or staff, particularly if the officers were armed. Ultimately, the institution is responsible for their actions. T4T firmly argues that arming police on school grounds and college campuses is *not* the answer. It is unsafe. Community building is the alternative to carrying a gun.

T4T's only option was to recruit local community members, along with the police department, and train them together through community-conscious, experiential learning exercises. Officers would have the opportunity to learn directly from the community they serve. In exchange, the community would learn more about the challenges that officers faced, how to engage with law enforcement, and how to hold rogue officers accountable. The collective goal was to provide a safe space to heal, share experiences, and build a collective vision for what community-conscious policing means to all stakeholders.

Amidst the Michael Brown protests, T4T invited the community to engage directly with police in Oregon. While the gap between law enforcement and communities of color was widening, T4T was working to close the gap. During a time when it was not popular to engage with police, T4T took that risk and felt pressured to do something proactive.

Hate Letter versus Inclusion

In 2012, Brandon served as a faculty member and administrator of student affairs at Oregon State University (OSU). His department supported more than 400 multicultural and international student-led organizations and clubs. In the women's center on campus, a threatening hate letter was found in a suggestion box in the women's restroom a week before winter term finals.

Below is a copy of the hate letter, including typos, sent to the women's center at OSU in 2014:

"Hello WC Staff,

I think that Black people belong on a noose. They need to be killed and lynched like old times so that they know their place.

I do not know why you have a black person in your midst, it is completely ridiculous that we are mixing races. I do not know how a black person can be a feminist or even call themselves educated. She belongs on the nose and should be lynched so that she knows who she is or where she comes from. We are letting black people invade our space and she dares support her director and GTA [graduate teaching associate] as if she mattered or even existed. She does not know that she is invisible; that she is fucking black and does not have a place here amoung the educated people at OSU. She better watch her back or she will end up on the noose. Again I believe that she would be lynched, black people are fucking stupid; those niggers don't belong amoung us; or at the Women center."

The letter was directed at the only African woman student who worked in the women's center, and it threatened violence against her and other Black students. Brandon served on the Bias Response Team in charge of addressing this matter. He assumed that the team would be working with students, staff, and law enforcement to solve this case and make the students feel whole. Instead, a group of executive-level administrators put forth every effort to protect the university at the expense of the victim.

As a result, the crime was never solved or reported as a hate crime. The victim was denied access to academic scholarships that she had earned, lost her financial aid, and worst of all, blamed for writing the hate letter found in the women's center. In response, Brandon continued his career in community and educational advocacy in Oregon.

Community Building

The president of the NAACP Corvallis/Albany Branch sent out an anonymous survey to figure out if other students or staff had also been victims of hate crimes. They needed to determine if the letter was an isolated incident or if there was a pattern of racism that had simply been ignored by police and the university administration.

The feedback T4T received was overwhelming and demonstrated a consistent pattern of racial behavior on or near campus by students, faculty, administrators, and patrol officers. Unfortunately, many of the students did not recall which law enforcement agencies had profiled or harassed them, which indicated to Brandon that there needed to be training that allowed individuals in the community to understand their rights, as well as have access to practical safe spaces to learn themes such as "How to Survive a Police Stop." These would be facilitated by BIPOC people who have been successful in responding to racial profiling and police misconduct. This is important for diverse impacted community members, so they know what information is most pertinent when filing a formal complaint after their civil liberties have been violated.

Five different law enforcement agencies exist in Corvallis. Their head-quarters are all in the same building. On top of that, the Department of Public Safety was also on campus. Brandon couldn't hold any particular law enforcement agency accountable. The group's collective efforts ensured that Brandon followed the DOJ's recommendation to contact local law enforcement in the case of an alleged hate crime. Brandon had previously met Chief Jon Sassaman at the NAACP branch meeting.

Sassaman came prepared with the data his department had collected regarding traffic stops, and he could statistically determine that racial bias wasn't present in his department. However, Brandon wanted to present the qualitative data he had collected from students, educators, and law enforcement. It was NAACP Corvallis/Albany Branch, OSU, and local police department's collective duty to ensure the safety of the students while on or near campus.

Chief Sassaman's quantitative analysis did not consider the qualitative factors. Brandon couldn't understand how a law enforcement agency could police itself without input directly from the people they serve. The seed was planted: police accountability also involved bringing diverse residents to the table to find out how residents wanted police to be trained.

Humanizing Collective Experiences

Hun and Brandon worked to connect the victim at the women's center with trauma support from a counselor who was also Black and advocated for the student's financial aid to be reinstated. By the end of Spring term 2014, she'd earned more than $20,000 in academic scholarships! The scholarships were based on her own merit and academic performance, not a result of the hate crime that had targeted her. More importantly, through the community building workshop, she was able to build alliances with CPD leadership and patrol members, and even build some camaraderie with many of the female officers.

Wearing her Muslim hijab made her feel like a target on the bus around town. As a result, she would walk for miles to avoid riding public transportation. Upon moving to more affordable housing off campus, she felt obliged to remove her traditional dress to safely get to and from school without feeling isolated or being harassed.

Out of everyone in the room, the person who most identified with her story of being a targeted African Muslim woman in rural Oregon was a White middle-aged woman who worked on parking patrol. The stories she told of how she was mistreated while ticketing illegally parked vehicles made many of the participants realize the harassment that some police feel.

Even though the officer owned a gun and could certainly protect herself if needed, these two people from very different backgrounds were able to find common ground. They empowered one another simply by sharing their respective stories in a brave space. For example one of the participants who self-identified as LGBTQ and a woman of color became a corrections officer based on the experience she had at the T4T workshop. By working beside local law enforcement, T4T was able to ensure a safe environment for underserved students that translated into increased student retention.

It should be noted that after T4T held Oregon State University accountable for this hate crime letter, the university received a national diversity award in 2018, 2019, and 2020 (OSU, 2020). The president, provost, and other academic leadership retired and improvements were made. More Black male leaders were hired on campus. This is the subject of the article, "Oregon State honored for the third straight year with national diversity and inclusion award" by Sean Nealon published by the OSU Newsroom on September 23, 2020.

Exercises

VICARIOUS TRAUMA

The information and subject matter contained within this book may cause vicarious trauma to the reader. To prevent that from happening, in acknowledgment of the triggering nature of this material, trauma, and healing, the first exercise is a tool to reestablish blood-flow to your frontal lobe:

THE RECOVERY BREATH

Perform this exercise before, during, or after stress or trauma occurs.

1. Exhale out of your mouth and fully clear your lungs.

2. Inhale through your nose for two counts.

3. Exhale out of your mouth for eight counts.

4. Repeat steps 2 and 3 nine times, or until you feel your heart rate slow down.

This exercise was taught by Master Heg Robinson at the Roxbury Taichi Academy in Boston, Massachusetts. It was then used in Greater Boston at Taireiki Wellness Center in general when providing wellness services and specifically at the beginning of individual and group session when treating victims of sexual assault. Often, participants were in an agitated or hyper-vigilant state after commuting through traffic and navigating their day. They reported racing thoughts and worries, and a general inability to calm themselves and relax. The defining feature of the "agitated" state was that it got in the way of work, school, and healthy relationships.

After performing the recovery breath for about five minutes, 75 percent of participants reported they felt calmer and less agitated. They said that their thoughts began to slow down and their worries seemed less urgent during and shortly after the exercise. When participants practiced regularly (every other day), they were able to maintain the benefits of the recovery breath a little longer each day, starting a new foundation of internal stability. This translated into an increased capacity to engage at work and home in a healthy manner for some participants.

Everyone reacts to trauma differently, but even the self-professed "hard-core" people experience its negative effects. As you read through this book, check in with yourself. Unresolved trauma translates into symptoms of unprocessed grief. Observe yourself as you read, and double your self-care routine, whatever it may be—stretching, herbal tea, exercise, prayer, art, nature.... This way, you can make it to the end of this book and carry this work forward however you can.

SPINAL TWIST EXERCISE

This exercise is one way to bring emotions back into balance. The proximity of your neck and upper back to your brainstem is such that when experiencing trauma or stress, tension, inflammation, dehydration, pain, or numbness usually occur in the neck , shoulders, jaw, and upper back. Gentle stretches allow your body to soften. Your relaxation response will stimulate your immune system and bring you some relief. Listen to your body as you do this exercise. If you have injuries, surgeries, conditions, or scar tissue, listen to your body and follow your doctor's advice. Only twist to 75 –80 percent of your threshold for mobility, pain, flexibility, or strength. Perform these steps slowly for safety.

1. Sit comfortably in your chair with your feet flat on the floor.

2. Turn to your right. As you turn, your legs remain pointing forward.

3. If you have a chair arm, grab the one to your right. If not, grab the right side of your chair, twisting your core and torso. Grab the back of your chair, if you can.

4. Come to a comfortable, sustainable position in your seated spinal twist.

5. Inhale gently and deeply through your nose, expand your abs and inflate your ribs.

6. As you inhale fully, expand your abs, inflating all four lobes of your lungs. Your abdomen should expand like a

balloon. Your belly button should move out, away from your spine, as the sides of your body and your lower back inflate. (As your diaphragm depresses during inhalation, your internal organs will receive a massage from your breath.)

7.   Exhale slowly and gently out of your mouth as you deepen your twists.

8.   Repeat this breath (steps 5 and 6) four to nine times, or for 60 seconds total. Continue to breathe until you feel your breathing deepen and your body soften.

9.   Slowly, gently unwind your body and return to the front.

10. Then perform your spinal twist on the left side.

11. Return to step 1 and replace right with left.

This breath produces an internal organ massage, freeing trapped emotional toxins, liquids, pollutants, nutrients, blood, and lymph fluid throughout your body was described by Timothy McCall, M.D., in his 2007 book *Yoga as Medicine: The Yogic Prescription for Health and Healing* published by Bantam in 2007. If you feel afraid, angry, frustrated, resentful, impatient, numb, apathetic, nervous, or sad, integrate this exercise. It will help get the liquid components of your emotions moving back into balance within your body.

DELIVERING A DEEPER TRAUMA HEALING PERSPECTIVE

It is human fragility that unites us. Humans are born utterly helpless. They depend on the kindness and love of others for their very existence. They all feel pain, and they're all going to die. Kemetic principles state that it is this fragility that unites humanity. While trying to heal rifts in the community between the police and the survivors of police brutality, it is important to understand this fragility is the commonality between people.

Following this train of thought, there are basic ways that the human body reacts to trauma and pain. David Emerson and Elizabeth Hopper, Ph.D., in their book *Overcoming Trauma through Yoga: Reclaiming Your Body*, published by the Justice Resource Institute, Inc., in 2011, state that certain parts of the anatomy and physiology govern trauma and stress responses.

Emotionally, the body cannot tell the difference between mortal danger and slight discomfort. An officer drawing his gun and pointing it at you, a nightmare, the painful memory of a dead loved one, physical discomfort like hunger, or low-grade headache can all register the same emotional response. They all trigger your stress, trauma, fight-or-flight, or tend-or-befriend responses in your anatomy.

As discussed in *Yoga as Medicine*, the reptilian brain, located at the brainstem near the base of the skull, is the command center for pain, stress, anger, and fear in the human body's trauma or stress response. When the reptilian brain is hyperactive, in the face of fear, stress, or pain, it shuts off your immune system, shuts down your stomach, stops blood flow to most of the frontal lobe, and prepares the body for survival by rapidly flooding the blood stream with various stress hormones. Some of these chemicals, like cortisol, are highly acidic and corrode soft tissues through your body. Sustained periods of pain, hypervigilance, or PTSD can cause cortisol, adrenaline, norepinephrine, and other hormones to circulate in your body for longer than they should.

One method for restoring this blood flow to the frontal lobe is breathing, which has already been discussed. Some people clench their jaw at night or during the day. Some people's neck pain and tension translates into migraines or tension headaches.

People who are used to being silenced, disenfranchised, talked over, and not heard often clench their jaw, causing pain and tension in their neck.

Some people don't suffer with active pain in their necks and shoulders. Instead they become numb. When your neck and shoulder region goes numb, it's actually more dangerous, because you can't feel injuries. This is true when it comes to emotions too.

Emotional numbness in police officers is a breeding ground for police brutality. When you do healing work on places in the body that are numb, you have to be very careful. Often, as part of the healing process, the numb places in the body will inflame and become painful as the nerve sensitivity, awareness, and proprioception return. Feeling pain is a necessary step in the healing process.

People who suffer from insomnia or racing thoughts often have neck pain or tension throughout their shoulders and upper body. The following is a series of neck stretches to relieve tension or pain from the base of your skull down to your upper back.

NECK EXERCISE

1. Sit up straight in your chair comfortably, with your feet flat on the floor.

2. Extend your right arm down towards the floor at a 45° angle.

3. Tilt your head to the left bringing your left ear toward your left shoulder. (You'll feel the stretch on the right side of your neck, in your right shoulder, down your arm to your fingertips, and up to your jaw, temple and eyes.)

4. Inhale gently through your nose expanding your upper chest and neck.

5. Exhale slowly from your mouth, fully clearing your lungs. Repeat this breath four to nine times. (Caution: do not force your head into the tilt. Instead, surrender to gravity without using muscle force.)

6. To come out of this pose, bring your chin to your chest and roll your head to the front. Bring your right hand back to your lap, then you should be able to bring your head up without any issue.

7. Repeat steps 2–6 on the opposite side, replacing "right" with "left" and "left" with "right."

8. Sit up straight in your chair.

9. Bring your shoulders back and down and hold them in this position for the duration of the next stretch.

10. While your shoulders are back, slowly lower your chin to your chest and feel the base of your skull, the back of your neck expand and stretch. Be gentle.

11. Hold this position and inhale into your upper back.

12. Exhale slowly from your mouth, allowing gravity to bring your chin down while your shoulders are back and down. Be gentle.

13. Repeat this breath (steps 11–12) four to nine times.

14. Return your shoulders to a normal position.

15. Move your head in a clockwise circle slowly three times. Try to move through all 360° of motion gently.

16. Inhale as your chin moves up.

17. Exhale as your chin moves down. Repeat this breath (steps 17 and 18) three times.

18. Then move your head slowly counterclockwise three more times. (Repeat steps 15–17, replacing "clockwise" with "counterclockwise.")

19. Bring your chin down to your chest; roll your head to the front.

20. Then bring your head back up to the center.

These exercises were used at a trauma healing seminar series for Boston Medical Center's Violence Intervention Advocacy Project (VIAP). VIAP employees respond to gunshot and stabbing emergency 911 calls. They arrive at the scene or in the emergency room and, depending on what is needed, provide victims of violence legal advocacy or social services. These workers regularly attend funerals for young adults and make trips to the city morgue to identify bodies, which is mentioned here to provide context of the sad, emotional environment in which they work.

One VIAP worker in particular lost a loved one to gang violence, merging his work and family life with tragedy. The result was persistent insomnia that lasted for six months. The group performed the above neck exercises during one of the seminar sessions and the insomnia sufferer fell asleep during the third neck circle to the left. He began snoring lightly when his coworkers gently teased him to wake-up, but he kept sleeping. He slept for 15 minutes as participants took a break.

HEALING EXERCISE FOR LACK OF SLEEP

As the discussion continues about what is essentially domestic peace building, it is important to talk about sleep. There's no symbolic metaphor to connect these two topics. In the past, when delving deeply into traumatic stories during in-person sessions, facilitators would pause to give participants a moment to engage in whatever self-care they needed to before moving onto the next topic. Sometimes this looks like a bathroom or coffee break. Participants can take a walk, call a loved one, or simply sit in silence to emotionally regroup.

Engaging in this triggering, difficult work has a high probability of causing poor-quality sleep for readers of this book. This could take the form of insomnia, sleepwalking, night-terrors, sleep-eating, nightmares, narcolepsy, or other issues. As the discussion of police redress moves forward and as people engage in actions to bring accountability, it's important to get a good night's sleep.

Sleep is a necessity of the human body. Trauma can disturb sleep and compromise the immune system's ability to heal during deep sleep, according to Dr. Timothy McCall. Most courts in the United States can deem you legally insane or mentally impaired and unable to make decisions if you've gone 48 to 72 hours with no sleep, and lack of sleep can cause severe cognitive issues if it persists. This next exercise is designed to nourish the need in all of us for a good night's sleep.

You may wish to read the exercise first in its entirety so that you don't have to read the book while you're falling asleep:

1. Clear a space for yourself large enough to lie down.

2. Gather some pillows, blankets, or other soft materials to make yourself comfortable.

3. Lie down so that you're comfortable.

4. Put your feet up. On the seat of a chair, on a couch, with your legs up the wall, or with your feet, lower legs, and knees propped up on pillows. This will take pressure off your lower back.

5. Do a scan of your body to make sure there's as little pain and tension up and down your spine and your limbs as possible. Be as comfortable as you can be.

6. Inhale gently through your nose, expand your abs and inflate your ribs.

7. Exhale slowly out of your mouth. Clear your lungs and relax your body.

8. Continue to breathe slowly and deeply four to nine times. (Repeat steps 7 and 8).

9. If you are still awake, release the tension in each body part as you go.

10. Release your scalp, face, tongue, jaw, neck, shoulders, arms, wrists, hands, heart, chest, back, spine, sides, abs, hips, glutes, thighs, knees, calves, shins, ankles, feet, and toes.

11. Then bring your mind to your heart.

12. Listen to your heartbeat in your chest.

13. Listen to your pulse throughout your body.

14. If your mind begins to wander, gently guide it back to your heartbeat.

15. Stay here for 15 minutes, if you can.

The emotional and physical benefits of a good night's sleep are too numerous to mention here. I'd like everyone participating in Community Conscious Policing to be well rested.

After almost all in-person gatherings stopped when COVID-19 made it unsafe, this exercise was delivered for lack of sleep online as a video via social media platforms. One recently widowed two-time cancer survivor and former attorney suffering from sleep issues reported that she fell asleep while performing the relaxing body scan from step 15 of the sleep exercise. She was able to sleep through the night soundly after that.

Institutional Inertia and Frozen Emotions: Figure Four Stretch

While working to overcome the institutional inertia and redefine police culture, be aware of inflexible, stuck thoughts or feelings you harbor personally. If they are ignored, they can show up in the physical body as sickness, behavioral misconduct, or impairing the ability to act professionally.

The next exercise deals with frozen emotions. When there's trauma, emotions can get frozen in your body. This can manifest or feel like impatience, frustration, resentment, annoyance at new ideas, or the feeling that you're not being heard.

Practically speaking, frozen emotions usually translate to lower back, gluteus, and hamstring stiffness or pain. When moving forward in this very demanding work, anticipate that officers, advocates, community members, decision makers, legal professionals, and people engaged in police accountability work will hit a point where frozen emotions show up in their physical body or in their work. It may cause some to quit.

Frozen emotions can express themselves in the form of impatience, resistance to change, not listening, shutting down, or remaining close-minded. It could show up physically in lower back pain, migraines, tension headaches, and hamstring stiffness. The following exercise is designed to deal with all of those things, so that one can unfreeze their emotions and continue to move forward in this process of empathy.

1. Sitting in your chair, cross your right leg over your left.

2. Extend your arms forward.

3. Slowly reach over your bent legs, towards the ground.

4. Listen to your body. Only go 80 percent into your tolerance for pain, flexibility, or strength.

5. Continue forward until you feel a stretch in your hips, thighs, and lower back. If you feel any pain or discomfort in your right knee, you have gone too far. Back off from the pose slightly.

6. Inhale gently through your nose, expand your lower back and your abs.

7. Exhale slowly out of your mouth.

8. Continue to breathe slowly and deeply 4 to 9 times.

9. Repeat steps 6 and 7.

10. Remain in this pose until you feel your back, hips, and thighs relax and your body softens, increasing your comfort in this pose.

Lower back pain and tension can affect your kidneys. According to Master Shou-Yu Liang and Wen-Cung Wu, who wrote *Qigong Empowerment: A Guide to Medical, Taoist, Buddhist, Wushu Energy Cultivation*, your kidneys govern listening. Lower back and kidney pain during this demanding process can impair your listening and your ability to move forward. For anyone suffering from lower back pain, frozen feelings, cognitive dissonance, impatience, or frustration, please use this exercise liberally.

The exercise was used from 2007-2014 at St. Francis House, the largest homeless day shelter in Boston. St. Francis provides social services during the day from 8 a.m. to 4 p.m., 365 days a year. The average person seeking services had been incarcerated for two–five years and homeless for more than 12 months. Thirty-five percent were veterans, 60 percent were victims of sexual assault or abuse, 45 percent struggled with drug addiction, and all of them had diagnosable PTSD.

During this 2007–2014 period, the Figure Four stretch was used with over 500 homeless individuals weekly as part of the Wellness Initiative at St. Francis House's Moving Ahead Program, a 14-week program designed to move a person from chronically homeless to housed and employed. The participants of this program reported that performing the Figure Four stretch released pain and tension that relieved their emotions and brought them back towards balance and calm. In more manic or impatient individuals, there was a calming effect reported. For others, it lessened anxiety and fear making social interaction and public speaking easier.

Success in this program was measured through job placement, which doesn't directly measure the effectiveness of the Figure Four stretch, but

68–72 percent completed the program successfully with employment that lasted for six–12 months.

The exercises helped heal trauma and calm emotions. One can then transfer a balanced emotional state to others, via the mirror neurons. Empathy is not a poetic concept. It is a biological function. The following is an exercise that amplifies compassion and gratitude.

Heart Light Exercise

The following exercise requires no mental or physical exertion. Perform all of the directions gently.

1. Sit comfortably in your chair and close your eyes.

2. Bring your mind to your heart.

3. Feel your heartbeat in your chest.

4. Once you can feel your heartbeat, visualize light shining in your heart.

5. With your imagination, see sunlight shining from your heart in all directions.

6. Hold this image in your mind and feel your heartbeat.

7. Visualize inhaling warm, gentle sunlight through your skin.

8. Relax as you exhale darkness from your body in all directions. (Imagine pain in the form of shadows, smoke, oil, or tar leaving your body.)

9. Continue this breath for three to five minutes. Stay longer if you'd like.

Master Healer Sokara Kamalisa taught this exercise during her Reiki and healing seminars at Oberlin College from 1999–2002. This exercise was used during weekly Trauma Informed Yoga classes at Tewksbury State Hospital, a psychiatric facility run by the Department of Mental Health in Massachusetts, from 2018 until the COVID lockdowns of 2020. Success is very difficult to measure in this environment because medical, disciplinary, mental health, and legal actions determine a person's ability to attend class and length of stay at the hospital. This made it difficult to perform data tracking.

However, the overwhelming response from the participants and the staff was that participants all benefited greatly from the exercises. Some students had isolated themselves from others until the yoga weekly classes. Some students who were victims of sexual assault while at the hospital found these classes to be one of the few safe spaces during the week. Students reported feeling much better after class and always requested additional classes.

Chapter 18

Challenges

CURRENT EVENTS AND MEDIA ATTENTION: DO THEY HELP OR HINDER WHEN BUILDING COMMUNITY BRIDGES?

The idea of a community-building workshop with law enforcement was frankly crazy, especially as other police shooting cases of unarmed Black men began to take over national media attention.

Data was collected from all 50 states to discover where and how law enforcement bridged gaps with the community during polarizing times. There were programs such as Coffee with a Cop, town hall public forums, or publicity stunts by organizations seeking to capitalize off the attention. However, none of them brought change in a way that seemed meaningful to survivors or in alignment with past community-led movements.

For this reason, the Community Conscious Policing workshops that T4T designed and implemented locally and statewide in Oregon were unprecedented in the state. From these experiences, T4T established a Police–Community Integrated Training and Education model that incorporates Community Conscious Policing workshops to bridge the gap between law enforcement and the community it serves during polarizing times.

Even in cities that reprioritize police funds to community-led initiatives and first responders, training and policy remains critical to maintain equity in power dynamics between first responders and victims in need of support.

Even when information is transferred from law enforcement to community-based first responders, there needs to be a process that ensures diverse residents who are impacted the most are at the design table contributing to what they want to see in first responders.

In Oakland in 2009, the cell phone video of Oscar Grant getting shot in the back while lying handcuffed on his stomach, surrounded by officers, set the tone for the next decade (Booker, 2020). The excuse the officer had given during trial was that he thought he had reached for his taser but pulled his gun instead by accident. The officer had made similar mistakes during his training.

In 2014, Eric Garner was choked to death on camera by the NYPD for allegedly selling loose cigarettes, a minor misdemeanor offense (BBC, 2019). In 2014, a 12-year-old named Tamir Rice was killed in an Ohio park while playing with a toy gun (Dewan and Opal, 2015).

In South Carolina in 2015, a Black man named Walter Scott was killed by Michael Slager, an officer who was also caught on camera planting evidence on the scene to support his bogus claims of feeling as if his life was in danger (Lartey, 2017). On camera, it's obvious that Scott was running in the opposite direction as he was being shot repeatedly by the officer.

On March 13, 2020, Breonna Taylor, a 26-year-old Black woman, was fatally shot eight times by the Louisville Metro Police Department in her own apartment after three plainclothes officers executed a "no-knock" search warrant at her residence. Breonna Taylor was an upstanding member of the community who worked saving lives as a first responder and emergency medical technician (Oppel, Taylor, and Bogel-Burroughs, 2021). She worked hand-in-hand with law enforcement on a daily basis, making this police murder that much more egregious.

On May 25, 2020, George Floyd, a 46-year-old black man, was killed in Minneapolis, Minnesota, by police officer Derek Chauvin, who knelt on Floyd's neck for eight minutes and 46 seconds in the middle of the street, despite being filmed by bystanders. Chauvin was protected by his fellow officers as he committed murder in public. The heinous nature of Mr. Floyd's murder and social media recirculating these images sparked protests, calling for the abolishment of police departments and the defunding of law enforcement agencies across the country, including major cities like Minneapolis and Los Angeles (Hill, et al., 2020).

Videos from cell phones are the modern-day "Bloody Sunday." The country responded in 1965 when images of peaceful protesters being treated very violently by law enforcement in Selma, Alabama, were broadcast on TV around the country (Klein, 2021). It was called "Bloody Sunday." Now, technology has given every person the power of video.

If a picture is worth a thousand words, then a video must be worth a million. The victims' voices, which had previously been silenced, can now be heard from beyond the grave. Protests are not just occurring in urban areas with larger minority populations, they are also occurring in New Hampshire, Maine, and in small towns throughout the United States. These protests occurred for months (Taylor, 2021).

Each incident highlighted biased policing practices nationwide. None of the police departments mentioned had training experience focused on racial equity and Police-Community Integrated Training and Education (P-CITE) quite like T4T.

How Does One Recruit 50–70 Community Members to Attend a Community Building Workshop?

The police are not capable of policing themselves, nor should they be allowed to. This system is not "broken." It is built this way on purpose, to benefit the few who sit anonymously at the top—just like its predecessor, the slavery system. It is also important to understand that elected officials and the legal apparatus of the United States alone is not capable of creating the systemic change that will reduce killings and brutalization by police officers.

Only the community, the people, non-officers, non-elected officials, the formerly disenfranchised, and the survivors of police brutality are qualified to initiate and oversee sustainable change in policing over the long term. Only with community in the lead, can we overcome institutional inertia that has resulted in so many deaths. Change can be sustained with transparent civilian oversight.

It is the community that has the power to hold police truly accountable. T4T is on a mission of peace. This is a time when every global supply chain has been disrupted by the COVID-19 global pandemic of 2020. The unity and community created by successfully undertaking T4T's mission in police departments, municipalities, and states is needed to address the collective crisis.

It was important *not* to focus solely on inviting community representatives or leaders. What cities often discover during times of crisis is that those who are recognized to be "community leaders" typically are not. Maybe they were in the past.

Black people are usually the focus of mainstream media as it pertains to police-involved shootings. Hun and Brandon are a part of the Black community already, so they don't have to "break in" or "target" communities for diverse outreach. They invite everyone as their neighbors to engage directly with the leaders in law enforcement who make the tough decisions regarding hiring, budget allocation, training, accountability, and equipment such as military-grade weapons and body cameras.

T4T trained the entire Corvallis Police Department including dispatch, administration staff, and parking enforcement on how to engage more consciously. The challenge Brandon was most concerned about was recruiting enough community participants, then having them evenly distributed throughout the four workshops. The first workshop was held during the day on a Tuesday, and the second on a Friday.

Recruiting for Tuesday while the community had to work would be Brandon's first challenge to overcome. People had to take time off from work and arrange childcare to attend. Participants had to figure out transportation, and T4T was not able to compensate them for their time. These factors are room for improvement in T4T conferences.

Facilitators understood the conditions were not perfect and thanked every participant who sacrificed to ensure that their voice was heard by law enforcement leaders. Without diverse community input from people who live closest to the pain incorporated into the fabric of public institutions, cycles of violence between police and community will continue. This is why police accountability and reform are not possible without revamping law enforcement training to center the experiences of people who traditionally have been most impacted by law enforcement violence, racial profiling, and police misconduct.

Hun and Brandon were able to use their personal networks to support T4T outreach efforts. Brandon's role as an officer in both the Oregon NAACP and the local Freemason Lodge helped Brandon to save money and find support for recruiting.

Ultimately, T4T recruited nearly 70 people to attend all four workshops in Corvallis. T4T divided the training into four smaller workshops to more evenly distribute community members and police officers. Even the chief attended, which made an incredible impression on everyone, especially Brandon. To provide a safe space, T4T kept group sizes under 50 people. The officers were paid and required to go by Chief Sassaman. It was clear that he was committed to the workshops and took an incredible risk to remain on the cutting edge of law enforcement practices.

It was a fraught time. Police departments in general were simply afraid to engage directly with community members in situations they didn't control.

At the training, police wore plain clothes and carried no weapons. They came to engage deeply with real people from different walks of life. As facilitators who were not law enforcement, this style of training took a great deal of trust to pull off, even the mayor signed off on the curriculum. Police-Community Integrated Training and Education (P-CITE) was a fairly new model at the time.

Corvallis Lodge #14, A.F.&A.M., must also be recognized, as my brothers served as gracious hosts to bring people together who would otherwise remain at a distance. The meeting place was one of the first buildings erected in the city downtown and definitely served a historical purpose that added to the ethos of community in our workshops. The lodge reminded us from whence we had come, how far we had travelled, but also how much further we had to go.

T4T convinced community members to take off from work, find a way to the workshop, and then engage with the local police department for free. In training workshops, facilitators always advocate for interpreters, a community stipend, transportation, food, childcare, and peer support. T4T works to be mindful of offering more than one event to be more inclusive of community members who face barriers to participate.

T4T resorted to the original organizing model of "Each One, Reach One, Teach One." In other words, Hun and Brandon mapped out everyone from their personal and professional networks who had a vested interest in this project for a variety of reasons. T4T recruited those individuals and asked them to find another who fit the same criteria.

T4T didn't utilize any social media or public outlets for outreach, because facilitators didn't want the event mistaken for a gimmick. It took roughly three months to recruit over 100 diverse, impacted community members. Of those, 70 attended.

Community organizations included were the Cambodian Association of Small Business Owners, Latino Police Commission, faith-based and community organizations, League of United Latin American Citizens (LULAC), Center for International Organizing, the National Women's Coalition, Safe Haven Mano a Mano Homefree, Visioning and Partnership Homeless Activities, Portland Community Peace Collaborative, Vancouver Police Chief's Diversity Advisory Board, various high schools from Portland, the state lodge, and the NAACP.

How Could We, as a Consulting Agency, Ensure All Participants' Safety?

During this time, the daily news covered protests against police nationwide and the state of emergency in Ferguson, Missouri. Some officers were terrified to sit in the same room or even talk to someone they had arrested in the past.

There was one Latino couple that was afraid to attend. Each of them had had a separate interaction with the police that did not go well. One of them filmed a police stop at a distance and was harassed by the officers. The other was stopped by a plainclothes officer one evening in front of her home and wrongfully detained.

At the time they had no open cases, but they had filed complaints with the police. Because there was no civilian review board in place, officers mishandled their complaints. Officers did not respect their privacy and these two individuals' names and addresses were made public, violating their confidentiality and privacy, making them afraid to attend.

The workshop did have a participant, called Jake for this story, try to call out a specific officer who he felt had unjustly arrested him in the past. This was a violation of the rules of the workshop, which Brandon had clearly laid out. (You can't speak directly to anyone in the circle, and you can't respond directly to what's being shared). To preserve the workshop's harmony, Brandon reminded the group of the ground rules and moved on without inviting the person back into the dialogue. Although Jake shared his grievances on the evaluation sheet later that afternoon, the officers appreciated that Hun and Brandon kept everyone focused on the goal to build community.

Brandon spoke to the attendee personally during the break to explain that the training could not be turned into a court hearing about his traffic stop. T4T was here to center the experiences of people who are historically abused by police brutality and systemic racism. Jake agreed to remain focused on the purpose and agenda. However, after another outburst, Brandon had to ask him to leave, which he did without pushback.

Ultimately, the goal is not to ensure that every voice is heard. Rather, it is to center the experiences of people closest to the pain. This means that time, attention, resources, and perspectives should focus on communities that have been impacted, oppressed, and disenfranchised throughout generations because of police brutality.

T4T designed exercises for this workshop that they have continued to refine. For example, many of the workshops culminate with a role-playing activity, depending on the topic. Facilitators ask the participants to take on two roles during the role-playing: observer and actor. This way, they can discover insights and learning opportunities in a real-life scenario by learning from the perspectives of others in the group or community who witness it. Usually, law enforcement only gets the perspective of the actor in a scenario, but needs the insights learned from other perspectives on the same situation.

Through the role-play, the group is able to press pause in a scenario and ask for collective wisdom from the group on how to navigate certain scenarios. This allows facilitators to process critical events and situations with less emotional attachment and glean the skills necessary to navigate a similar situation in the future. When the participant switches roles to become the actor in a scenario instead of the observer, actors can then practice lessons they learned from the group to prepare for authentic community engagement that potentially could save a life. Brandon and Hun believe that role-playing has been critical in helping both law enforcement and community members in understanding each other's perspectives, even if they ultimately disagree.

To learn more about the community members that had been recruited, T4T had people fill out applications to attend the workshops. The process helped when seats were limited. In the first round of applications, T4T asked for basic demographic information.

Triumphs

The triumphs were too numerous to count. For example, officers felt comfortable sharing their experiences of losing partners in the line of duty. Community participants got to hear about the stresses of overwork, the challenges of being available for family outside of work, and not being able to go out in public without worrying about seeing someone they arrested. They also learned directly from officers how to engage with them in an optimal way. Community participants got to know local patrol and parking enforcement officers on a first-name basis and connected with them through shared experiences that were revealed throughout the day. In addition, colleagues within CPD learned more about one another.

Above all, Corvallis police officers were able to learn more about the complexity of the constituents they serve. For example, they learned about the differences and overlap between international students, refugees, immigrants, migrants, and undocumented community members. CPD learned how many community members share similar feelings for different reasons. For example, as a Black man growing up in Oakland, Brandon will always be threatened any time a police car gets behind his vehicle.

A parking enforcement attendant who works with law enforcement also feared getting pulled over. As a single mother, receiving one ticket could prevent her from being able to provide her kids with a birthday party or Christmas presents. Every day, she lives with this fear of some unexpected event happening and not being able to provide for her family. One of the African students said that she routinely had the police called on her when she would jog around her neighborhood and some of the Black men had been followed by slow-driving patrol cars as they left campus.

Facilitators also had a lesbian college student who had recently been arrested for domestic violence. Through tears, she shared it was the officer who had first made contact that helped her become whole from the experience and rebuild her life. She had come that day to thank the officer who arrested her for the counsel she provided while escorting the student to jail, and for representing her story so accurately in the police report. This young woman had completed all of her stipulations resulting from that arrest, and now works as a corrections officer in the same county. The workshop exposed her to a new career in law enforcement that she may not have otherwise considered.

Participants who attended left feeling healed, connected, and part of a bigger community that was entirely vested in its healthy future.

Our workshops took place the week before the verdict came out in Ferguson. It determined that Officer Darren Wilson would not be charged for killing Michael Brown, even though Brown was unarmed and, according to witnesses, had his hands raised in the air in surrender (Horwitz, Berman and Lowery, 2017).

As a result of the workshop, activists and community members had an opportunity to express themselves in a meaningful dialogue that reduced tensions citywide. While other towns held protests after the verdict, Corvallis experienced no violence and relatively little pushback from the community. Through the workshops, CPD had already demonstrated their commitment to what T4T collectively defined as Community Conscious Policing.

Shortly after the Ferguson verdict, a group of predominantly white college students protested in front of the Corvallis police station. Due to the proactive approach to community building prior to the verdict, the NAACP and Corvallis Masons were able to unite and share with protesters that the police department should be supported, not antagonized. Protesters left and shortly afterwards, the entire town of Corvallis celebrated the positive publicity.

The 13th Amendment of the US Constitution made it legal to treat criminals like slaves. Criminals are denied civil, human, voting, and jury rights. They are denied housing, employment, loans, and education because of their criminal status. They are denied these rights because of the label "criminal" instead of the label "Black."

Growing up in California during the crack epidemic, Black and minority community members were used to police corruption in cases like the Los Angeles Rampart, Oakland Riders scandals, and the Iran Contra Affair. It was understood that certain law enforcement teams, programs, and officers were simply not to be trusted. Some officers were even known in the community to employ "street justice" tactics. These tactics were brutal in the community. The introduction of the battering ram and "War on Drugs" ushered in a whole new wave of law enforcement corruption and police misconduct (Murch, 2015) that made Brandon weary of all police, simply because of what Brandon had observed as a child. He heard stories of his grandparents, aunts and uncles, dad, and older cousins. And then he began to experience the racial profiling and racial discrimination first-hand.

This message below was written by Brandon's aunt. "Mom" refers to Brandon's grandma, "daddy" refers to Brandon's grandfather, and "grandpa" is Brandon's great grandfather.

> "Yeah. We are Choctaw. Mom's Mother is Choctaw, from Rain, Louisiana. Daddy's Father is Cherokee, Grandpa's Dad is a full blooded Indian (Seminole). The Seminole tribe's origin was Alabama and Georgia, then relocated to Florida. The Seminole call themselves the "Unconquered People," as they are descendants of just 300 American Indians who managed to elude capture by the US army in the 19th century.
>
> Grandpa's mother was nine years old when Lincoln freed the Slaves. Grandpa was born in Mississippi but raised in Baton Rouge, Louisiana. Grandpa lived with us from when I was 15 and then he died in 1965. Uncle Bud and Buster are dark like Grandma: Mom's Mother."

Brandon refused to pass on the issue of systemic racial profiling and police brutality down to his son. It stops with T4T, and it must stop now. Brandon's family tell him about how his dad used to organize the community against police brutality while working as an Assistant to the Mayor of Oakland, even before Brandon was born. Community Conscious Policing runs through Brandon's veins, and it is why he dedicated this book to elders like his father and the Black Panther Party for Self Defense also founded in Oakland.

Chapter 19

Solutions

FBI NATIONAL ACADEMY ASSOCIATES REQUESTS COMMUNITY CONSCIOUS POLICING

The captain of the City of Corvallis Police Department, David Henslee, participated in the Community Building workshops. Facilitators did not know at the time, but he and Chief Jon Sassaman were both members of the prestigious FBI National Academy Association, which is the training arm for law enforcement organizations worldwide. In 2015, Dave served as the vice president for the Oregon chapter, and he was charged with hosting the Annual Spring Training for all state law enforcement agencies.

By 2015, protests and states of emergency had spread to New York (for the NYPD killing of Eric Garner), Baltimore (where Freddie Gray had died handcuffed in the back of a police van), and Homan Square in Chicago (where the police department interrogated witnesses and shackled, beat, and tortured potential suspects without booking them into jail). The nation was hurting and desperately looking for an innovative approach to law enforcement training that incorporated community building with an equity focus.

A few months after the workshops, Dave called and said that he and his wife would like to come to Hillsboro to meet Brandon and Hun. They agreed to meet at a local Korean restaurant, where all parties could break bread and catch up.

Over dinner, Dave said that he'd recommended T4T to the FBI National Academy Associates (FBINAA) for their annual spring training. The board wanted an opportunity to engage with community members versus focusing on tactical training. This would be an opportunity to reach most state law enforcement agencies in Oregon. Also, participants at the spring training included senior officers who had served as police officers for at least a decade, and most of them consisted of leaders—chiefs, training lieutenants, and sheriffs.

After dinner, Hun and Brandon accepted the challenge of hosting the annual training for the Oregon Chapter of FBI National Academy Associates. First, they needed to identify a few challenges before they could develop an action plan. The couple insisted that the training be referred to as a workshop, since they don't use slides or classroom-type lectures. And they needed to think about how to recruit for and facilitate the event.

Their team used various sources of data collection to compile a report that would demonstrate to the FBI National Academy Associates how they'd execute the training.

T4T was ultimately tasked with training 100 chiefs and sheriffs, along with 50 community members, for eight hours. The curriculum had to be modified to provide a safe space in a large auditorium with a stage. First, they wanted to spend the morning working only with law enforcement, to prepare them for the community-building portion of the workshop. T4T focused on best practices in Community Conscious Policing, where the officers were able to build together on themes such as recruitment and retention, building effective teams, and community engagement.

Because every officer present is in a leadership role and highly experienced, it was imperative that community members were diverse, yet brought a level of engagement that would match this caliber of talent.

Mobilizing the Community

Mirroring their efforts in Corvallis, Hun and Brandon began with their personal networks and invited them to attend. They then trained those who agreed to be mobilizers to recruit neighbors, community members, and coworkers who were invested in proactive solutions. Together, they identified communities that were rarely invited to engage with police and identified organizations that could provide access in an authentic way.

T4T focused outreach on Black, Indigenous, Latinx, and people of color who had historically been impacted by Oregon Exclusion Laws and other tactics of state and federal legislation. Historically, these tactics have compounded the impact of racial profiling and police brutality with living in an isolated rural community. In Oregon, these laws were established in the 19th century to create a White utopia for early settlers. This subject matter is detailed in Imarisha Walidah's Oregon Black History Program in Portland (Nokes, 2020).

Brandon has found that every community contains mobilizers or local agencies that are well-connected and in tune with the issues most pertinent to local law enforcement and the community it serves. These are the people who T4T wanted to be involved in a training effort like the one they were mounting.

The training was hosted on a Wednesday in Salem, which is at least an hour drive from the major cities of Eugene, Portland, or Corvallis, where colleges are located. Here, too, community members T4T recruited had to volunteer their time, find their own transportation, and take time off from work or school to travel nearly an hour or more to participate.

T4T recommends that community members be compensated for their insights to provide an ongoing dialogue. Facilitators didn't know until the event if these barriers would prevent people from participating: Law enforcement was on edge, and news of the protests was galvanizing communities nationwide. Many events during this time were being shut down by protesters. Law enforcement was afraid to speak with community members for fear of being misunderstood. Community members who had experienced trauma for generations were tired of talking.

It was possible that police in the training room carried concealed weapons. It was possible that community members had a legal right to carry concealed firearms. In retrospect, facilitating a space between law enforcement and community members during such a polarizing time could be called ill-advised. But the curriculum was community-led, so facilitators could reorient the power dynamics and police were not in charge of the space. Non-law enforcement community members had drafted the curriculum. As a result, each experiential learning exercise centered the experiences of the people closest to the pain. Brandon personally had connected with each participant prior to the event.

Everyone was motivated to get something out of the time together, which set the tone for some real talk about real life and making a real change. This later became the inspiration for the motto at T4T, which is "Real Life, Real Talk, Real Change." Shortly thereafter, Corvallis PD hired their first Black police officer. Brandon likes to think that the series of training workshops prepared the department to diversify and become more racially conscious.

Time and Financial Constraints

By the time T4T followed up with the board to execute the contract, facilitators only had three weeks to plan and execute. Due to the event's size, T4T recruited Angela Berkfield, a consultant from Vermont's Act For Social Justice. She specializes in beginning conversations with White people about what it means to be anti-racist.

Next, they hired Alejandro Juarez, a Latino man with experience organizing around marriage equality for LGBTQIA+ communities and communities of color. For technical and staff support, they hired Nate Okorely, who works as a full-time engineer in San Diego.

Finally, Hun co-facilitated for the afternoon community-building section, even though she was eight months pregnant with twins. Everyone admired her dedication, leadership, and service. We'd spent most of the budget on facilitators who specialize in the content area and called upon volunteers like Nate and FBI National Academy Associates board members to assist in recruiting community members.

Angela, Hun, and Brandon had met at their alma mater, the School for International Training Graduate Institute. Collectively, T4T has more than

75+ years of direct experience and education working in African American, African, Latino, Native and Asian communities.

Counter-Narrative of Policing

It is doubtful that many law enforcement agencies truly understand that for some community members, police do not represent the "rule of the law." Their badge represents a form of domestic terrorism to people like Brandon, who are more likely to be killed by a cop than a foreign extremist terrorist organization like Al-Qaeda.

Chapter 20

Lessons Learned

Our team was fortunate to have spent so much time learning from the Corvallis PD. While the department's size isn't comparable to a big-city precinct, it is similar to many college towns and rural law enforcement organizations that face challenges centered around recruitment, retention, diversity, and community engagement. Due to the support of the city's mayor and police chief, T4T was able to gain complete access to the department, its officers, administration, dispatch, and parking enforcement.

Hun and Brandon mediate those whose opinions may be contradictory to their own perspectives. Law enforcement is not trained to "open up." T4T's 21st century conscious-based leadership recognizes everyone as a living being, and facilitators want to minimize the negative effects of the activities on the environment they leave after engaging. The choices, rules of engagement, and disengagement made by law enforcement are more complex nowadays.

The discussion returns here to the fact that implicit bias training doesn't change institutional, systemwide behavior. And the linear training methods and tools are no longer effective for dealing with various communities across Northern America, due to the complexities of identity in the 21st century.

For example, due to a variety of factors such as politics, global warming, immigration, and technology, neighborhoods and communities are becoming even more diverse. According to Valarie Wilson for the Economic Policy Institute, the majority of the American working class will be people of color by 2032 (Wilson, 2016). As a result, law enforcement will need to be able to engage across linguistic, socio-economic, and cultural differences in order to provide public safety in a way that is healing-centered, trauma-informed, and culturally responsive.

Community Conscious Policing workshops create real opportunities for officers to practice what they have learned through role-playing and scenario-based learning in the academy, without the fear of having to use their weapons in protection of themselves or someone else.

In these training sessions, participants can identify potential "bad apples," or identify patterns or practices from outdated training that may show up as a liability on the street. When an officer chooses not to engage or doesn't quite have the skills to engage with diverse communities effectively, community members need to be able to provide this information to law enforcement leaders.

Today, T4T is training law enforcement how to connect with people that they may not have otherwise connected with prior to the workshop. The skill to survey one's own biases requires specialized training and another way of processing information. Then facilitators teach the officers to search for similarities they may share with others rather than the differences.

By doing so, T4T anticipates fewer liabilities and lawsuits that center around racial profiling, and fewer reports of police misconduct for those agencies that complete the certification. Even better, T4T hopes bonds will be forged between officers, leadership, and community members. This will proactively reduce violence, trauma, and pain for all involved.

According to the evaluations taken from workshops conducted in 2014, 85 percent of participants agreed that the workshops were helpful and 88 percent of participants would recommend the workshops to others. Nearly all of the participants wanted more Community Conscious Policing workshops so they could engage with one another more deeply.

In 2021, T4T is proposing that Community Conscious Policing be fully funded to facilitate a cultural paradigm shift in law enforcement on city, county, and state levels nationwide. They have empirical evidence, quantitative statistics, and qualitative feedback from evaluations administered after the Community Conscious Policing workshops.

Both community and law enforcement were overwhelmingly in support of wanting more opportunities to engage in this style of training. T4T doesn't offer a solution such as "abolish" or "defund" the police, but they do offer a process to ensure that the people closest to the pain and most impacted by law enforcement violence are at the design table of what policing should look like in the 21st century.

T4T has proven the concept of Community Conscious Policing to be relevant and in demand, but funding should be provided to sustain a cultural paradigm shift of a law enforcement organization T4T partners with over time. Brandon learned that everyone in T4T workshops is simply responding to whatever trauma, pain, or unfortunate circumstance has impacted their daily lives. Some endure more than others, while others don't recognize the privileges society unjustly affords them.

Reactions to Trauma

It's worth it to extend the discussion about trauma here instead of glossing over it because it's universal and affects everyone adversely. Delving more deeply into understanding trauma will also help one understand the emotional costs for the individual. We'll also better understand the public health cost for communities created by police violence and lack of accountability.

There are several reactions to trauma. Some are unique to the individual and others are common throughout humanity. In his April 17, 2010, lecture entitled, "The Condolences: Stories from the Iroquois Delivered During the Native Awareness," at the Maine Primitive Skills School in Augusta, Maine, Michael Douglass taught that trauma causes your perception to clog and your eyes and ears to play tricks on you. Auditory hallucinations occur in extreme cases, causing you to mishear all news as bad news, and compliments as insults. Your fears take over your eyes, causing you to see your enemies in every silhouette and shadow. You may actually see and hear things that are not there—or worse, you may inaccurately judge the behavior of others through this lens.

Mirror issues can occur when a person is traumatized. Have you ever been scared of your own reflection? Have you ever looked in the mirror and not recognized the face that you see? Or have you avoided the mirror altogether for weeks at a time? Do you spend all of your time looking into the mirror, hour after hour after hour? All these are common reactions to trauma.

Stomach issues are also a common occurrence. Constipation, food allergies, upset stomach, acid reflux, ulcers, stomach cancer, irritable bowel syndrome, food sensitivities, emotional eating, sleeping eating, nocturnal eating, anorexia, bulimia, or other complications can occur when you're traumatized.

When a person is exposed to pain, they usually try to stop it. In the case of trauma, when the pain can't be stopped, people will try to numb it or avoid it. Often you see people reaching for addictive substances or spending way too much time watching TV or on the internet. Some will use any chemical or engage in any activity or behavior in a manner that distracts them from the pain they feel internally. It could be gambling or sex addiction, but usually you see trauma at the root of these.

Sometimes, people dealing with trauma turn on their allies. Everyone has someone in their corner who has given to them genuinely. When you find yourself turning on that person, becoming mistrustful of them, insulting them, attacking them or worse, this is a symptom of unprocessed grief.

Self-sabotage is another sign of trauma. People identify a goal, and then, as they near achievement, they suddenly flake out, get busy, and have very poor excuses for why they didn't follow through. You can see this clearly with people who are looking for a job: they spend months in a job search process, get the offer letter, and then don't show up on the first day of work. Anyone can do this after having enough averse traumatic experiences.

When a person is traumatized, they can struggle to maintain the basic functions of life. Washing dishes, washing clothes, answering the phone, opening mail, showering, brushing their teeth, taking care of cuts and bruises—everything becomes too hard.

Trauma can affect a person's speech, too. Someone might have outbursts of negative speech or steer conversations toward negative aspects. This type of person usually repeats lies and rumors excessively, getting into a lot of arguments even though they're not trying to. Someone going through a divorce could have every intention of remaining calm while having a discussion with their ex-spouse. Despite their best efforts, they may utter an insult and regret it immediately. The traumatized individual has no control over what they're saying. Even if they want to say something nice, even if they want to be silent, even if they're telling themselves to speak positively, still negative speech comes out.

When this happens, a person can no longer trust his own thoughts, feelings, and perceptions. The opposite can also happen: a person adopts silence and isolation as a coping mechanism.

Trauma strips people of their own internal resources.

Take a professional chef, for example. Once traumatized, he can no longer show up to work. They can no longer cook even though they may have a restaurant chain franchise that's very successful. They can't seem to summon the emotional energy to show up.

Landlords who own multiple properties go through trauma, and they can't seem to rent those places anymore. In extreme cases you'll see suicidal behavior. Cutting or hurting oneself, making suicide threats or suicide attempts, whether as a cry for help or with intention. They're all symptoms of unprocessed grief and trauma.

Homicidal behavior usually has the same causes. Homicide and suicide are two sides of the same coin. That coin is a lack of reverence for life, your own life or the lives of others. To clarify, this does not mean that if someone is suicidal, they could easily also be homicidal. This means that at the core of both of these states is *lack of reverence for life*. This is the most dangerous place to be in and these are the most dangerous people to be around.

An individual usually doesn't display all the symptoms, and individuals may not display all of the symptoms in one lifetime. Symptoms of unprocessed grief come in groups and clusters. A person isn't just experiencing stomach issues, people experience stomach issues, nightmares, and fear of going back to work.

These are examples of what someone who's responding to trauma and pain looks like. Trauma and Post Traumatic Stress Disorder (PTSD) are part of the hidden costs of non-Community Conscious Policing that affect the families and communities of survivors and victims of police brutality.

When officers are uneducated about trauma and PTSD, they also go untreated, which makes them more likely to act out brutal tendencies while policing and cuts off their empathy when dealing with people exhibiting symptoms of unprocessed grief (Brott, 2019).

Strength can be found when both community members and law enforcement officers overcome the oppression or barriers that have impacted them the most. Discovering the similarities in one another is the most powerful part of the workshop's experience.

How to Improve

Currently, T4T offers a variety of tailor-made services for government, educational institutions, and civic and nonprofit organizations to make changes in vision, mission, policies, procedures, and practices that increase accountability and end loss of life. T4T is currently based in the Pacific Northwest but looks forward to expanding nationwide. As a result of the community affiliations, professional networks, and international background through the School for International Training, T4T is poised to become a global leader in Police–Community Integrated Training and Education (P-CITE) through their Community Conscious Policing workshops.

Ideally, the innovative T4T training protocol should be implemented for cadets or any entry-level candidates in law enforcement agencies. This training would be longer and more intensive if offered through a semester-long curriculum where community and law enforcement can engage more than once.

Workshop themes initially would begin with examining, assessing, and dispelling personal biases. It would involve developing mock scenarios to see what triggers a particular resentment of a group (race, gender, sex, religion, or origin). One exercise that facilitators have used to confront bias is called, "The Gallery Walk." Facilitators break community members and law enforcement up into small groups and position them around the entire room. They provide each group with a big sheet of butcher paper and markers with themes across the top. Each team represents various groups within the community. For example, one poster board reads, "immigrants," another reads, "Black people," another reads "transgender," and others read "police officers," "homeless people," "people experiencing a mental health crisis," and so on.

Each group wrote down stereotypes that they had heard about, not what they particularly believed in, on the butcher paper and posted them on the wall when they were done. In silence, they walked around. The groups slowly read each paper posted on the wall that had the stereotypes listed of each group.

The first question to the group was, "Do you believe in the stereotypes that you read on the wall?" Pretty much everyone agreed that they did not believe in the stereotypes on the wall. The second question was, "How did they make you feel as you read them?" They all agreed that it made them feel horrible to see how others can be viewed in the community.

The final question was, "Well, how did these stereotypes get into this room?" It was at that moment that it began to dawn on the people in the room that, although participants may not *personally* accept these stereotypes, they have somehow permeated participants' consciousness. *They* brought the stereotypes into the room. It was necessary to own the biases that participants contributed to in order to build a new vision of shared community.

There was one more lesson to be learned. One attendee was not able to participate in the gallery walk due to a temporary disability. It was at this moment that T4T recognized the workshop had not considered people with disabilities while trying to design experiential learning exercises. Moving forward, this would never again be overlooked.

T4T workshops delve deep into examining what makes one feel uncomfortable and why. They discuss issues of race and identity. They then deconstruct the concept of "to protect and serve" with a strong focus on service. Initially, some of the training would involve only members of law enforcement, while some would involve members of the respective local community.

As stated, the training and facilitation methods are based on experiential learning. Expanding T4T on a regional and then national scale will require them to increase the number of facilitators and educators in T4T practices. It also will enable T4T to improve recruitment, retention, best practices, and community engagement.

T4T's objective is to create a partnership with a government or national law enforcement agency that can provide the resources needed for T4T to continue the community-building workshop on a larger scale. This partnership would enable T4T to perform with greater intensity.

T4T is also seeking to establish relationships with community colleges, police academies, universities, law enforcement training facilities and community-based organizations interested in guiding this work in their local areas.

Chapter 21

Case Study #9: Unitus Community Credit Union

Institutional accountability is not the burden of law enforcement alone. The next case study involves Unitus "Community" Credit Union in Beaverton, Oregon, which worked with their security guard to call the police on Brandon. The armed security guard closed the drive-thru-line early, and then tried unsuccessfully to bully Brandon when he attempted to ask why the guard had closed early. Brandon noticed the guard wasn't wearing a mask during the COVID-19 shutdown putting life in jeopardy through neglecting quarantine protocols.

Brandon was able to call the security company and bring accountability to his situation in terms of the security guard. Ironically, it is the bank who has yet to take corrective action for its involvement with its employee and branch manager who are both complicit in the police being called on Brandon.

He wanted to let this go, but he was shopping for a home at the time. Every time he spoke with Unitus, the frustration came back up and that's when he knew that the case needed to be made public. This incident is a perfect example of how white supremacy is perpetuated systemically, and why people are going public with real life stories now to enter the national discourse on ending unjust police violence.

The public needs to know the truth about these kind of racial profiling situations. Institutions need to make corrective action fast to avoid causing

COMMUNITY CONSCIOUS POLICING

further harm, trauma, liabilities, and loss of communal trust. T4T is standing its ground against *all* forms of violence, especially racism.

Brandon was told that the branch manager of Beaverton was also present as he was being profiled outside, yet no one did anything at the Beaverton branch to diffuse the situation. This is troublesome, especially in today's political climate where Black men are murdered by police on camera in broad daylight regularly without justification.

Brandon was investigated like a criminal. The drive-thru bank teller and the security guard, both White, were wrong in how they escalated the situation by calling the police. He simply was trying to make a deposit before the close of business.

Instead of answering his question, the security guard, who was not wearing a mask, tried to bully Brandon. The guard prompted the Unitus drive-thru teller to call the Beaverton Police Department. Luckily, Brandon, via T4T, had trained the Beaverton Police Department in 2015 at the Department of Public Safety Standards and Training, which enabled the officer to see right through the racist request for police assistance.

The security officer at the Beaverton branch lied, saying that Brandon had made a hand gesture in the form of a gun and threatened the guard. This was a clear case of racial profiling and misconduct by the security officer. It is not merely an opinion, but a diagnosis of problems that may be systemic and more deeply rooted. Brandon was more than qualified to make these assessments. The police officer who came out to "investigate a crime" agreed that there had been no valid reason for law enforcement to be called out during COVID-19 for this situation. This situation was completely unnecessary, discriminatory, and could have gotten Brandon killed.

The assistant manager of Brandon's home branch in Tanasbourne was on the phone with him while he was being questioned by police. The manager could also serve as a witness, because he heard the incident as it was happening and apologized profusely to Brandon. The Tanasbourne employee stayed on the phone with him the entire time while the Beaverton Police detained him, demonstrating true leadership during a critical situation.

The Beaverton regional manager did listen to Brandon about what had occurred and how it was retraumatizing for Brandon, but this manager only took a few notes. All he did was take a few notes from Brandon's story and forward them to security relations at Unitus. What a waste of time and resources. Brandon deserved better as a long-term contributing member of Unitus.

The regional manager didn't even remove the security officer from the premises while this was being "investigated," because the same security officer was still working at the Beaverton Branch when Brandon returned. He'll never forget it, because the same security guard added insult to Brandon's injuries when he referred to Brandon as , "Bud," as though he is not a human being, business owner, and a professional.

As a minority business owner who trains law enforcement, a family man, Tanasbourne, Beaverton, resident at the time, member of Unitus, and a well-respected community leader, this situation remains very traumatic for Brandon. He looks forward to hearing how Unitus plans to make him whole. The incident made Brandon ask himself, "Is there any diversity in the regional or executive levels of Unitus?" Based on his personal experience, he doubted it.

Brandon has since made peace with the security company after speaking with its CEO. After doing some research, Brandon discovered that the security company was owned by one of his friends and fraternity brothers. Brandon was assured that the security guard would be swiftly held accountable for his actions and this would never happen again. Unitus isn't as progressive as it promotes itself to be, unfortunately. It's revealing how they were complicit in what happened to Brandon and unwilling to take corrective action with their employees. Brandon's instincts tell him that there is more going on behind the scenes at the Beaverton branch, which resulted in him being racially profiled and harassed by their security officer. What Brandon endured is not acceptable, and he looks forward to hearing from Unitus regarding a peaceful resolution to this urgent issue.

So far, Brandon had to fix his own problem and there needs to be some accountability and training brought to Unitus leadership and the Beaverton Branch employee(s) who were also complicit in what happened to Brandon with the security guard. The security company is the only one who has owned their part in all of this and then did something to change their behavior. What about Unitus? Brandon applied to be on the Board of Directors in order to advise the CEO and his predominantly white executive team on how to avoid similar situations from happening again.

Chapter 22

Recommendations

Up until this point, this book has focused on the lived experience of the author, his shared professional expertise, and the wisdom of their teachers. The topic of Community Conscious Policing and police accountability is larger than T4T. According to the National Conference of State Legislatures, 40 states already have passed police reform laws, including banning choke holds. A few have done away with "qualified immunity", which shields officers from accountability when they abuse power.

There are other efforts towards police accountability, reductions in brutality, equity, and inclusion that should be mentioned during a discussion of Community Conscious Policing.

When working with decision-makers, legislators, police officials, or when strategizing unique solutions for your own community, the following recommendations can be useful tools. Be careful of inauthentic or corrupt behavior and evaluate your implementation efforts for effectiveness regularly. Corrupt behavior is defined by the The Great Book of Divine Ordinances. The 77 Commandments provide a clear measure of what human behaviors produce destructive results and leave no middle ground between what is acceptable and what is not. Following the Commandments is considered the perfect model for humans to follow.

For example, Commandment 54 states, "Thou shall not be impatient," so when plans and actions are made, impatient attitudes and subsequent hasty actions are identified and stopped whenever they occur. As mentioned in chapter 17, The second Commandment states, "Thou shall not intrigue by ambition," so monitor people and decision makers involved. Be sure the ambition of individuals, whether financial, political or otherwise, doesn't interfere with efforts to make police reforms.

All of the Commandments do not make sense in every situation. Generally, one or two of them will apply to a situation, giving a clear indication of what to do and what not to do. This will help produce outcomes that don't inadvertently or indirectly cause harm.

1. Implement a Ceasefire

The 2013 Oakland Ceasefire program was implemented in response to 710 shooting victimizations in 2011. A law enforcement, public health, community partnership used this Group Violence Reduction Strategy to address the underlying issues of poverty and inequality that make people commit crime.

In "Oakland Ceasefire Impact Evaluation: Key Findings" (2018), Anthony Braga, Gregory Zimmerman, Rod Brunson, and Andrew Papachristos report this mixture of law enforcement, community mobilization, and social services decreased the shooting victimizations 52.1 percent, to a low of 340 in 2017.

2. Couple Police with Mental Health Professionals

Repeatedly, T4T saw that pairing behavioral health clinicians with police officers produces an effective form of Community Conscious Policing. This recommendation reduces the workload for law enforcement officers. When Crisis Intervention Team (CIT) training is mandated for all police officers, call center operators, and jail personnel, and give judges the authority to get defendant's mental health treatment, significant statistical reductions in arrests and recidivism rates will result.

In "The Four Best Examples of Police and Mental Health Response," published in Rave Mobile Safety on November 21, 2019, examples can be seen in the police departments of Miami, Florida, beginning in 2010; in Denver, Colorado, in 2017; in the 2015 Ostling Act of Washington State; and in Houston PD's Mental Health Division in 2015. For sure the CAHOOTS model implemented by Eugene PD is worth mentioning. They helped to design the MACRO mental health response team for Oakland PD as well. On January 1, 2021 the Bay Area Rapid Transit (BART) Board in California as part of its Roll Call for Introduction 20-832: Progressive Policing plan also announced it will be hiring social workers instead of police officers.

These recommendations include creating a gate in the 911 dispatch system that identifies and redirects mental health crisis-related calls to a group of licensed mental health workers trained as first responders for that police district.

The author is aware that CIT training alone without other T4T curriculum elements is ineffective because traditional CIT does not address racial injustice or accountability.

3. Measure LL and S1: Legislate Civilian Oversight of Police

After years of work, city charter amendment Measure LL in Oakland, CA, established the Police Commission to oversee the police department's policies, procedures, and general orders that govern use of force, profiling, and general assemblies.

The Commission established a Community Police Review Agency (CPRA) to investigate all complaints involving use of force, in-custody deaths, profiling, and public assemblies. After completing its investigation of a complaint, the Agency submits its findings and proposes discipline to the Commission and the chief. This measure empowered the commission to hire and fire the police chief.

Further strengthening Measure LL, in 2020 Oakland, California, Measure S1 2020 empowered the Police Commission (Commission) to separate from the city administration, hire its own attorneys, and reestablish the Office of Inspector General (OIG) under Commission oversight instead of the Chief of Police oversight. The OIG reviews CPRA investigations then reports to the Commission and City Council making the civilian Commission more independent. The OIG now oversees Oakland's compliance with Measures LL and S1. Measure S1 also allows more time for CPRA investigations, expands CPRA access to police files, and provides funding for CPRA to hire its own lawyers. The cities of Austin, Texas and Berkeley, California also have strong examples of civilian oversight of police.

4. Protect Those on Parole and Probation

Generally, people on probation or parole have no rights and are subject to searches at any time and for no reason. The Oakland Police Commission in 2019 limited these powers, requiring a reason before conducting a search according to Rashida Grinage, a long-term critic of the OPD who wrote, "Oakland Police Commission Passes Search Protections For People On Probation or Parole" for *Oakland News Now*.

5. Grant Public Access to Hidden Police Records

As talked about in Chapter 1, police often hide, redact, destroy, or otherwise obfuscate from the public a good amount of data. Internal affairs records, personnel files, misconduct records, complaint files, and other information never sees the light of day.

SB 1421, the California bill that legislates the "right to know about serious uses of force and proven police misconduct legislation," also known as the 2018 Peace Officer: Release of Records Bill, gives the public access to police investigations, findings, and discipline regarding deadly and serious uses of force (California Legislative Information). The release of records includes officer misconduct cases involving proven sexual assault against a civilian. It also extends to cases of proven dishonesty in the investigation, reporting, and prosecution of crimes, such as perjury, planting, or destroying evidence.

6. Stop Broken Windows Policing

"Broken windows" policing, a theory that promotes maintaining order through increasing arrests for minor offenses to prevent serious crimes (CEBCP 2021), is just an excuse for law enforcement to use profiling and stop-and-frisk tactics on Black and Brown people, especially in "inner cities."

When speaking to decision-makers, encourage them to remove all rhetoric relating to broken windows policing from legislation and policy documents. Law enforcement must end unjust tactics related to enforcing broken windows policing in your jurisdiction to eliminate the possibility of more police killings.

7. Don't Arrest Children through Schools

The school-to-prison pipeline, a set of racist policies and practices beginning in the 1970s, still systematically moves

Black and Brown boys from schools through social services to prisons (Justice Policy Institute 2015).

The Obama administration tried to use the Department of Education's Civil Rights Division to change harsh school discipline and policing policies that disproportionately impact students of color (Blad, 2016). In Denver, Colorado, the 2010 Advancement Project used informal classroom meetings, victim impact panels, and restorative conferencing to stop the arrest of children (Unidos and Advancement Project).

Even though the title of this recommendation is "Don't Arrest Children through Schools," officers shouldn't be arresting children *at all*. Anyone and everyone should be willing to move heaven and earth with all resources possible to ensure that child arrests don't happen anywhere.

8. Create Alternative Courts and Restorative Justice

Drug courts, mental health courts, homeless courts, veteran's courts, domestic violence courts, community service sentencing, and treatment instead of sentencing have all been used in jurisdictions across the US. These methods have all been used to divert people away from prisons to the services they need.

Between 2006–2014, Massachusetts opened a variety of these courts. Many people who would have been incarcerated received alternatives to imprisonment via the Massachusetts Specialty Courts (Mass.gov).

Restorative justice is a method of criminal justice that focuses on the offender providing restitution to the victim and community as opposed to focusing on punishing the offender at the community's expense. In "Restorative Justice in the States: An Analysis of Statutory Legislation and Policy,"

Sandra Pavelka provides an extensive review of restorative justice legislation throughout the U.S. It's worth examining the laws in other states to find ones that you could replicate in your area.

9. Community Service for Police

Mandate police cadets to volunteer with local community organizations while in training. Each quarter, they should rotate to a new local agency to serve and learn cultural proficiency and humility. Cadets in training would also gain insight into the struggles, triumphs, holidays, and cultural strengths of residents who may be new to them.

10. Train Communities

Train local communities in capacity-building, legal redress, and educational advocacy. This way, they'll be equipped to hold local politicians, rogue police officers, and institutions that demonstrate bias or racial profiling accountable.

Examples include the USC Class Action victory on Los Angeles' controversial gang injunctions (the elimination of gang injunctions), Thames Valley Police, and Thames Valley Sexual Assault Prevention Group. (These last two are UK-based.)

11. End Laws and Injunctions against "Gangs"

Laws, injunctions, and policies that target gangs often enable racial profiling and brutality. These laws call people of color gang members to justify acts that restrict civil liberties. These laws allow officers to make arrests based on a person's appearance or the color of the clothing rather than investigation or evidence of crimes.

Laws, injunctions, policies, and tactics targeting gangs should be removed and stopped. In 2018, Chief United States District Judge Virginia A. Phillips barred the LAPD from enforcing injunctions against gangs, extending her 2017 ruling in the 2017 court case the Youth Justice Coalition v. City of Los Angeles.

12. Declare Racism a Public-Health Crisis in Your Jurisdiction

Encourage your town, county, city, or state public official to make a public written declaration of racism as a public health crisis. In that declaration they should outline their understanding of the problems in the entities over which they have authority.

Then, with as detailed and long-term a plan as possible, the declaration should outline short- and long-term concrete, evidence-based measures to eliminate racial bias in the practice of medicine.

Recognizing racism as a threat to the health and well-being of people of color fosters dialogues on racism as a public health concern. It can end racial discrimination in medical care and prepare future physicians to be advocates for racial justice.

The American Public Health Association has compiled an extensive list of cities, towns, municipalities, and states that have made declarations. They also provide links to those declarations at: https://www.apha.org/topics-and-issues/health-equity/racism-and-health/racism-declarations.

13. End Violence against Women

On September 19, 2018, the U.S. Department of Justice (DOJ) awarded $240 million dollars in grants to improve public safety in American Indian and Alaska Native Communities. It should have been billions of dollars which leaves a great opportunity to make efforts to increase this funding to billions. The Office of Justice Programs, the Office on Violence Against Women, and the Office of Community-Oriented Policing Services provided the funding.

Funding was allocated to the following measures. Each tribe chose different measures in the following list to suit their needs. You'll see alternatives to correction, wellness, healing, and protection for women funded by the U.S. DOJ in the list.

1. Public Safety and Community Policing
2. Comprehensive Tribal Justice Systems Strategic Planning
3. Justice Systems and Alcohol and Substance Abuse
4. Corrections and Correctional Alternatives
5. Violence Against Women Tribal Governments Program
6. Children's Justice Act Partnerships for Indian Communities
7. Comprehensive Tribal Victim Assistance Program
8. Juvenile Healing to Wellness Courts
9. Tribal Youth Program

14. Record Gun-Pointing Incidents

Require cops to notify dispatchers after officers point a gun at someone. Supervisors should have to review, record, and report gun-pointing incident data. Departments also should develop training on when to point a weapon.

The 2018 court case of Illinois v. Chicago resulted in "The Chicago Consent Decree of 2018," an extensive, detailed example of police reform and accountability. In its 236 pages, it details Gun-Pointing Reform among many other aspects of police accountability and Community Conscious Policing.

There are still questions about the implementation and evaluation of all of these measures, especially in light of police killings as of August 29, 2020. As discussed earlier, reports aren't always accurate.

However, the decree still remains an outstanding piece of police reform. The measures it contains could be studied and implemented in your jurisdiction as appropriate.

15. Bring Accountability to Immigration

The implementation of deportation practices is where immigration becomes police brutality. Recently, lawsuits and court orders have been used to stop these practices.

U.S. District Court Judge Ketanji Brown Jackson wrote an extensive opinion stopping "expedited" and "fast-track" deportation in the court case Make The Road New York v. McALeenan in 2019. This 126-page opinion is a great resource for communities plagued by immigration officers.

Any time you see people in chains and cages with guns pointed at them, you should think of brutality, terror, and killings. *My Asian Americana*, a Studio Revolt project featuring Kosal Khiev and others, tells the stories of Cambodian-Americans ordered back to Cambodia by U.S. deportation. Outsourcing police brutality to immigration can no longer be tolerated.

16. Training and First Aid to Deadly Force Victims and Independent Investigations

Initiative Measure No. 940, the Washington State Law Enforcement Training and Community Safety Act (2017), requires violence deescalation and mental health training for officers. It requires them to render first aid to deadly force victims, and mandates independent investigations of deadly-force incidents.

In regard to the use of deadly force, advocate for the imposition of as many restrictions as possible on officers. Apprehension of suspects in 2020 doesn't require lethal force. Technology has provided plenty of non-lethal options for most situations that cops encounter.

17. Eliminate the Use of Electronic Monitoring (EM)

In 2019, the Mandatory Supervised Release Reentry Freedom Act of Illinois (HB 1115) banned the use of EM for those on probation, parole, and those who have completed prison sentences.

Typical EM devices are waterproof GPS-tracking ankle bracelets that notify officers directly. Companies often charge monthly fees to the person being monitored, further burdening families.

These devices increase incidents of police brutality in general. Every GPS "violation" or malfunction of the monitoring device triggers a law enforcement response and the possibility of another killing.

18. Fund Ex-Offender-Run Programs

Find funding for ex-offender-run programs that work directly with individuals with multiple gun charges, open cases involving firearms, or gun convictions.

These programs work best when police involvement is limited to enabling programs with funding. Programs run by the police always have problems gaining credibility in the streets when they ask people to trust them and participate.

Former offenders run the program and programs should be fully funded and long-term, five years or more.

Evidence-based programs build on attempts to address a participant's underlying need for services while helping them find a job or business opportunities. Participants are given small business grants in addition to full-time (35 hours per week) work, along with an array of social services. These programs focus on incorporating small businesses and understanding trauma healing.

Good programs are trauma-informed, using culturally relevant models based on Kemetic (Ancient Egyptian) and indigenous principles. Participants are also taken on trips abroad to change their perspectives and enrich their lives. AdvancePeace.org in Sacramento is a good example of an ex-offender-run program.

19. Toronto Listens to Black People

When municipalities, cities, and states listen to Black people, positive change occurs. Forty-one years of reports on racism were compiled and presented to Black communities in Toronto to let the people decide which recommendations would have the greatest impact.

In 2017, Toronto held 41 community conversations led by the city, in accountable partnership with Black community organizations. The result was the 2017 Toronto Action Plan to Confront Anti-Black Racism, a five-year initiative to end racism in Toronto. It passed unanimously.

Sections 16-18 of the action plan focuses on police reform. They eliminate "carding" as a policing practice, another "stop and frisk" policy. To increase transparency, the action plan mandated reporting of racial information in policing.

The city also created a Community Police Hate Crimes Advisory Committee and convened a Community and Police Eliminating Anti-Black Racism Team (CAPE-ABR Team). Dissemination of "know your rights" information was expanded, and community engagement was advanced as an alternative to policing. Alternatives to incarceration, such as restorative justice models, were developed and implemented with Black elders.

20. Create a Unique Action

TheMarshallProject.org is a database of thousands of criminal justice articles compiled since 2014. It's a beautiful website that puts information in a user-friendly format. It's a great resource for articles on mental health, police reform, police accountability, police tactics, and use of force.

21. Aviation-Style Safe-Proofing for Police

Michael Scott, former police chief and currently a professor of criminology and criminal justice at Arizona State University, suggests that when a cop kills, experts should humbly comb through the scene to find the cause and implement measures to prevent the next incident.

In aviation, this process is so effective that there are almost no plane crashes involving major airlines in the U.S. Why doesn't some comparable system exist in policing for every killing and incident of brutality? The reason is perfunctory policing.

Tony Cheng in "Input without Influence: The Silence and Scripts of Police and Community Relations," writes that perfunctory policing can be seen "where officers superficially comply with procedural requirements of a program or practice, but resist substantive changes in performance—leaving

residents to shoulder the consequences of police inaction."
Overcome perfunctory policing and implement safe-proofing
for law enforcement killings.

22. Make Police Violence a Public Health Issue

The American Public Health Association issued the policy "Addressing Law Enforcement Violence as a Public Health
Issue" in 2018. This policy was designed to drive the content
of legislative and regulatory recommendations. It includes
evidence-based rebuffs to arguments opposing addressing
law enforcement violence.

The action steps of the policy include making death or
injury by law enforcement reportable to the CDC. The steps
that follow then necessitate research, funding, and measures
to address this new statistic. This policy also urges legislative bodies to eliminate legislative provisions that shield law
enforcement officers. Lawmakers are urged to reduce police
militarization, swat teams, and swat team deployment.

Finally, the policy demands full public disclosure of all
investigations into officer brutality and excessive force. Any
associated recordings should be deemed public property.
The policy includes 136 references to help you as you craft
similar actions.

23. Dismiss Marijuana Charges

Many states have some form of policy for recreational,
medical, or decriminalized marijuana use. However, in the
race to consume THC, business interests forgot Black and
poor people who are still in shackles for possessing the prod-
uct in many states.

What an insult to those who are incarcerated for marijuana possession to know that American businesses are now

profiting from the same medicinal crop that landed them in prison. Let's vacate marijuana charges from people's records and release them from imprisonment. When looking at marijuana legislation, laws only mean justice when they vacate criminal records. Judges in Seattle, Washington, seem to agree.

On September 11, 2018, the municipal court of King County made a motion to dismiss possession of marijuana charges. Court orders seem to be a place where accountability is possible when legislation is not forthcoming or perfunctory policing and police brutality are resilient.

24. Reduce and Limit Use of Force: "Reasonable" to "Necessary"

When you examine the use-of-force documents in your jurisdiction, look for a "reasonable" standard—it means officers can kill without accountability even when there is no threat and alternatives to deadly forces are available.

Leaving this license to kill unaddressed means police killings will continue. The correction is to change the "reasonable" standard to a "necessary" standard.

A "necessary" standard means that officers must exhaust all available alternative options before using deadly force. It limits the use of deadly force to situations in which there is an immediate threat to life, and no alternatives are available. AB 392: The 2019 California Act to Save Lives is an example of this type of legislation.

25. Police Where You Live

In so many cases across the US, cops live in different cities or states than the one they work in. This is overwhelmingly the case in inner cities and impoverished areas. The "us versus them" mentality that is reinforced when cops come from outside of the communities is a toxic soup that feeds police killings.

Kazi Toure is an advocate, activist, ex-political prisoner, and keynote speaker in Boston. Regarding police accountability and reform, Toure says that police should live in the community where they work. In this way, officers can know, understand, and respect people from lived experience.

26. Removing Exceptions

Up until this point, these recommendations have been examples of laws that enshrine strong corrective actions. This method has flaws. Research reveals that the resiliency of the underlying structures is responsible for police killings.

For example, California Assembly Bill 32 Chapter 739 Section 2 Title 9.5. 9501 states, "Except as otherwise provided in this title, a person shall not operate a private detention facility within the state." Sections 9502-9505 then lay out the numerous exceptions. The enumeration of exceptions is many times longer than the ban, to the point that it is questionable if this ban will have any effect. Strive to remove exceptions from accountability and reform measures.

27. Return Indigenous Authority

Prosecutors, judges, police chiefs, legal professors, criminal justice educators, training lieutenants, officers, city councilors, congress members, governor, mayors, select boards, legislators, town managers, presidents, CEOs, and world leaders should give political power back to the traditional indigenous emperors, kings, and chiefs. These are the sentiments echoed in Prophet Naba's *Philosophy Podium* and by the Ayni Institute, a Boston-based nonprofit organization working to preserve Indigenous Peruvian Spirituality under the direction of the Peruvian Shaman Don Carlos.

28. Justice for the Disabled

According to the "THE RUDERMAN WHITE PAPER ON MEDIA COVERAGE OF LAW ENFORCEMENT USE OF FORCE AND DISABILITY: a Media Study (2013-2015) and Overview" by David M. Perry PhD and Lawrence Carter-Long, a third to half of use-of-force incidents involve a disabled individual.

Garner, Powell, Anderson, Gray, and Bland were not just African Americans; they were disabled African Americans.

Eric Garner, *who was killed on July 17, 2014, had diabetes, sleep apnea, and asthma. Freddie Gray, killed in Baltimore, had lead poisoning. Sandra Bland had depression and epileptic seizures. Kajieme Powell, who died at the police station, and Tanisha Anderson were also disabled. They had schizophrenia or bipolar disorder.*

Commit to justice for all people with disabilities—in lockdowns, in shelters, on the streets, visibly disabled, invisibly disabled, sensory minority, environmentally injured, and psychiatric survivors.

29. Ban Traffic Stops

Traffic stops shouldn't be conducted by law enforcement officers anymore and should be seen as an indication of bad policing. Traffic stops are dangerous for everybody involved. The drivers driving around the police that are in the way, the person who is stopped and put in close proximity to weapons and lethal training, and the officer that has to put himself in harm's way to affect the stop are all put in danger.

Nobody is served by traffic stops. Machines that don't blink can detect and send tickets via the mail for speeding, inspection violations, registration violations, moving violations, and excise taxes better than human officers. Most things that officers could do on a traffic stop can now be automated removing the bias from the traffic stops altogether.

Officers, agents, and deputies have unsolved cases in every zip code including crimes against women and unsolved murders. Time wasted on traffic stops would be better used on unsolved cases than on traffic enforcement activities that can be automated. This is not science-fiction, on February 21, 2021 Berkeley, CA already passed a law eliminating traffic stops. (City of Berkeley). A note to town administrators, leaders and executive branch decision-makers, automated traffic stops kill less innocent people and have less liability than stops by officers.

30. Limit Collective Bargaining Powers

"Prohibiting a law enforcement agency from negating or altering certain requirements or policies through collective bargaining" and "requiring a police officer to take certain steps to gain compliance and de–escalate conflict under certain circumstances; requiring a police officer to intervene to prevent or terminate the use of certain force by a certain police officer; requiring a police officer to render certain first aid to a certain subject and request certain assistance at a certain time". Maryland Police Accountability Act 2021.

31. Don't Jail People for Insufficient Bail Funds

On March 25, 2021 the Justice J. Cuéllar of the Supreme Court of California ruled in the case of Kenneth Humphrey, case number S247278, that it is unconstitutional to hold people in jail just because they can't afford bail. "No person should lose the right to liberty simply because that person can't afford to post bail. ... The common practice of conditioning freedom solely on whether an arrestee can afford bail is unconstitutional."

32. End Qualified Immunity

The New York City Council on March 25, 2021 voted to end qualified immunity for officers. This means that NYPD officers are no longer protected from civil lawsuits for police actions including, "establish a local right of security against unreasonable search and seizure and against excessive force regardless of whether such force is used in connection with a search or seizure ... the person would be able to bring a civil action against the employee or appointee, as well as against the employee or appointee's employer". The New York City Council Int. No. 2220-A.

33. Publish Misconduct Records

In March of 2021 New York City's Civilian Oversight Review Board published the misconduct records of 83,000 officers over the objections of NYPD's Police Union. This database can be found on it's website. Since then the NYPD has responded by publishing its own police misconduct database which can also be found on its website.

Implementing Recommendations

Any place where you see human effort, there's a possibility that it is being corrupted by the evil side of human nature. In the discussion about Community Conscious Policing, the corruption looks like racism and brutality, a continuation of police terror.

Any suggestions need to be taken with this grain of salt. One will have to constantly evaluate the quality of one's own efforts, the efforts of other people involved, and what one is doing so that efforts don't slip into performative activism.

Performative activism is defined as systematically performing acts that on the surface appear to be anti-racist, that are actually just to cover or continue unjust, racist practices, and behaviors. Remain ever vigilant at each meeting and in each interaction of the possibility of performative activism.

When reading the recommendations, look at the references cited. Read those materials and *their* sources. This process will give you the raw data, statistics, intellectual, and historical background you'll need to speak with confidence and intelligence about each recommendation.

Public officials, public servants, and law enforcement officers work for the people and the communities they serve. As a person and community member, and for these reasons alone, you should feel empowered to speak to any official, public servant, or law enforcement officer, and instruct them on how to best serve you.

Feel free to call, text, email, send a letter, or knock on the door of your officials, public servants, and law enforcement officers to discuss and begin the process of implementing your Community Conscious Policing recommendations.

They will either tell you, "No," or give you an enthusiastic ,"Yes, please help us." In the case of yes, bring this book with you. It's a good place to start and browsing these recommendations with decision makers should be enough to begin.

Conclusion

This book is designed to empower people who have survived racial profiling and police misconduct. They are descendants of African people who introduced the principles of order and harmony to humanity. This book is also for oppressed people everywhere regardless of what racial-ethnic categories and classifications have been assigned to those individuals by government entities. It is time to create a world that is in harmony for humanity.

For White "allies" and "accomplices" who stand beside the oppressed in the struggle for basic human rights, this book provides some context into the daily trauma experienced as a result of racial profiling and police brutality. For activists and advocates, there are insights from lived experience that may bring some clarity on strategies that have proven effective to thrive while living under this pressure.

For readers interested in law enforcement careers, this book provides a perspective that simply is not offered in current police training models. Engaging with diverse communities is a privilege that should never be taken for granted.

Any reader who believes their neighborhood, community, city, county, state, or country could benefit from Community Conscious Policing is invited to contact T4T and your local public officials to request a workshop or consultation.

REFERENCE LIST

abc7. 2016. "Family claims off-duty OPD officer terrorized them." https://abc7news.com/oakland-police-officer-cullen-faeth-resident-olga-cortez/1218137/.

American Public Health Association. 2018. "Addressing Police Violence as a Public Health Issue, Policy 201811." https://apha.org/policies-and-advocacy/public-health-policy-statements/policy-database/2019/01/29/law enforcement-violence

Alexander, M. 2012. *The New Jim Crow: Mass Incarceration in the Age of Colorblindness*. New York: The New Press.

Ali, D. 2017. "Safe Spaces and Brave Spaces: Historical Context and Recommendation for Student Affairs Professionals." *NASPA Policy and Practice Series* 2. https://www.naspa.org/images/uploads/main/Policy and Practice No 2 Safe Brave Spaces.pdf.

Allen, D. 2021. "A Forgotten Black Founding Father." *The Atlantic*, March 2021. https://www.theatlantic.com/magazine/archive/2021/03/prince-hall-forgotten-founder/617791/.

Alliance for a Just Society. 2006. "Listening Sessions Report: A Community and Police Partnership to End Racial Profiling." allianceforajustsociety.org/wp-content/uploads/2010/04/2006-1004 Listening-Sessions-Report.pdf

Alvarez, L. and C. Buckley. 2013. "Zimmerman Is Acquitted in Trayvon Martin Killing." *The New York Times*, July 14, 2013. https://www.nytimes.com/2013/07/14/us/george-zimmerman-verdict-trayvon-martin.html.

American Friends Service Committee. 2021. "Popular Education(*)." https://www.afsc.org/resource/popular-education.

Andrew, S. 2020. "This town of 170,000 replaced some cops with medics and mental health workers. It's worked for over 30 years." CNN, July 5, 2020.

https://www.cnn.com/2020/07/05/us/cahoots-replace-police-mental-health-trnd/index.html.

Asare, J.G. 2019. "Diversity Trainings Usually Fail — Here's What You Can Do To Create Lasting Changes." *Forbes*, September 27, 2019. https://www.forbes.com/sites/janicegassam/2019/09/27/diversity-trainings-usually-fail-heres-what-you-can-do-to-create-lasting-changes/?sh=44cded795241.

Ballotpedia. 2016. "Oakland, California, Civilian Police Commission, Measure LL, November 2016."

https://ballotpedia.org/Oakland,_California,_Civilian_Police_Commission,_Measure_LL_(November_2016).

Bartlett, T. 2017. "Can We Really Measure Implicit Bias? Maybe Not." *The Chronicle of Higher Education*. https://www.chronicle.com/article/can-we-really-measure-implicit-bias-maybe-not/ .

Bazelon, E. 2020. "Police Reform Is Necessary. But How Do We Do It?" *The New York Times Magazine,* June 13, 2020. https://www.nytimes.com/interactive/2020/06/13/magazine/police-reform.html.

BBC News. 2019. "Eric Garner: NY officer in 'I can't breathe' death fired." https://www.bbc.com/news/world-us-canada-49399302.

Bible Hub. "Isaiah 60:7." https://biblehub.com/isaiah/60-7.htm

Book, Brakkton. 2020. "California District Attorney Says Probe of Oscar Grant Killing Will Be Reopened." NPR, October 6, 2020. https://www.npr.org/sections/live-updates-protests-for-racial-justice/2020/10/06/920895464/california-district-attorney-says-probe-of-oscar-grant-killing-will-be-reopened.

Blad, E. 2016. "School Civil Rights Took Spotlight Under Obama." *Education Week*, May 2016. https://www.edweek.org/policy-politics/school-civil-rights-took-spotlight-under-obama/2016/05.

Braga, A. A., G. Zimmerman, R.K. Brunson, and A.V. Papachristos. 2018. "Oakland Ceasefire Impact Evaluation: Key Findings." Witness LA, August 2018. https://witnessla.com/wp-content/uploads/2018/08/oakland_ceasefire_impact_evaluation_key_findings.pdf .

Brott, A. 2019. "Healthy Men: Why are we ignoring the epidemic of white male suicides?" Medical Xpress, October 2019. https://medicalxpress.com/news/2019-10-healthy-men-epidemic-white-male.html.

Brizendine, L. 2010. *The Male Brain.* New York: Broadway Books.

Bryan, B. 2014. "Old attitudes and new beginnings: The Philadelphia police and MOVE: 1972-1992." Temple University diss. https://search.proquest.com/

openview/cb52dee07bc6c4419ef115f72bca9743/1.pdf?pq-origsite=gscholar&c-bl=18750&diss=y.

Budryk, Z. 2019. "NYPD substantiated zero incidents of biased policing in five years: report." The Hill. https://thehill.com/blogs/blog-briefing-room/news/450696-nypd-substantiated-zero-incidents-of-biased-policing-in-five.

CALEA. 2021. "About Us." https://www.calea.org/about-us.

California Legislative Information. 2018. "Senate Bill No.1421." https://leginfo.legislature.ca.gov/faces/billTextClient.xhtml?bill_id=201720180SB1421.

Center for Evidence-Based Crime Policy (CEBCP). 2021. "Broken Windows policing." https://cebcp.org/evidence-based-policing/what-works-in-policing/research-evidence-review/broken-windos-policing/.

Cheng, T. 2020. "Input without Influence: The Silence and Scripts of Police and Community Relations." *Social Problems* 67, no. 1. https://doi.org/10.1093/socpro/spz007.

City of Berkeley. 2021. Special Meeting eAgenda, February 23, 2021. https://www.cityofberkeley.info/Clerk/City_Council/2021/02_Feb/City_Council_02-23-2021_-_Special_Meeting_Agenda.aspx;)

Crime Report, The. 2020. "Massachusetts Drug Lab Scandal Expands With New Probe." https://thecrimereport.org/2020/12/18/massachusetts-drug-lab-scandal-expands-with-new-probe/.

Criminal Justice Policy Research Institute. 2011. "Decreasing Crime by Increasing Involvement: A Guidebook for Building Relations in Multi-Ethnic Communities." https://www.pdx.edu/cjpri/sites/www.pdx.edu.cjpri/files/Decreasing_Crime_By_Increasing_Involvement.pdf/-_f.

Cullen, J. 2018. "The History of Mass Incarceration." Brennan Center for Justice. https://www.brennancenter.org/our-work/analysis-opinion/history-mass-incarceration.

Dewan. S. and R.A. Oppel. 2015. "In Tamir Rice Case, Many Errors by Cleveland Police, Then a Fatal One." *The New York Times,* January 23, 2015. https://www.nytimes.com/2015/01/23/us/in-tamir-rice-shooting-in-cleveland-many-errors-by-police-then-a-fatal-one.html.

Douglass, M. 2010. "The Condolences: Stories from the Iroquois." Native Awareness II, Maine Primitive Skills School, Augusta, Maine, United States.

Dorn, A. 2017. "Johnson Says Oregon DOJ Didn't Show 'Loyalty' In Civil Rights Case." OPB.org. https://www.opb.org/radio/programs/think-out-loud/article/oregon-civil-rights-attorney-settlement-erious-johnson-interview/.

Dubois, S. 2016. "Portland police chief retires amid inquiry into shooting." AP News, June 27, 2016. https://apnews.com/article/c0130c3fb5c440b79fabffb-6dae7f21f.

Ellis, R. 2017. "Man fatally wounded by deputy; family says Facebook Live captured chaos." CNN, March 18, 2017. https://www.cnn.com/2017/03/18/us/facebook-live-killing-tennessee/index.html.

Emerson, D. and E. Hopper. 2011. *Overcoming Trauma Through Yoga: Reclaiming Your Body.* Justice Resource Institute, Inc., Boston, MA and North Atlantic Books, Berkeley, California.

Emoto, M. 2005. *The True Power of Water: Healing and discovering ourselves.* Beyond Words Publishing, Inc., Hillsboro, Oregon.

Estes, A. 2021. "Almost a decade after Annie Dookhan and the state drug lab scandal, the fallout is growing." *Boston Globe*, January 1, 2021. https://www.bostonglobe.com/2021/01/01/metro/nearly-decade-after-annie-dookhan-state-drug-lab-scandal-fallout-is-growing/.

Evans, Alonza Tehuti. 2017. "Social Impact of Prince Hall Freemasonry in D.C., 1825-1900." Library of Congress. https://guides.loc.gov/prince-hall-free-masonry/videos.

Federal Bureau of Investigation (FBI). 2021. "COINTELPRO." https://vault.fbi.gov/cointel-pro.

Feuer, A. (2017) "Death of Pioneering New York Judge Is Ruled a Suicide." *The New York Times*, July 26, 2017. https://www.nytimes.com/2017/07/26/nyregion/judge-sheila-abdus-salaam-suicide.html.

Forscher, P. et al. 2019. "A meta-analysis of procedures to change implicit measures." *Journal of Personality and Social Psychology* 117, no. 3. https://doi.org/10.1037/pspa0000160.

Franklin, B.C. 1931. "The Tulsa Race Riot and Three of Its Victims." National Museum of African American History & Culture. https://nmaahc.si.edu/object/nmaahc_2015.176.1.

Franklin, D. 2018. "Deaf man given $175,000 settlement after claiming Oklahoma troopers used excessive force during arrest." Oklahoma News 4, February 19, 2018. https://kfor.com/news/deaf-man-given-175000-settlement-after-claiming-oklahoma-troopers-used-excessive-force-during-arrest/.

Gillespie, E. 2015. "Vancouver police strive for diversity, not for animosity." *The Columbian*, August 16, 2015. https://www.columbian.com/news/2015/aug/16/vancouver-police-strive-diversity-animosity/.

Gottbrath, L. 2020. "In 2020, the Black Lives Matter movement shook the world." Al Jazeera, December 31, 2020. https://www.aljazeera.com/features/2020/12/31/2020-the-year-black-lives-matter-shook-the-world.

Grabowski, S. and G. Tortora. 2003. *Principles of Anatomy and Physiology*. New York: John Wiley & Sons, Inc.

Grinage, R. 2019. "Oakland Police Commission Passes Search Protections For People On Probation or Parole." Oakland News Now, April 12, 2019. https://oaklandnewsnow.com/oakland-news/oakland-police-commission-passes-search-protections-for-people-on-probation-or-parole/19225/.

Hadley, G. 2017. "Police told her, 'No more of your drama, OK?' Then she and her son were killed with an AK-47." *Miami Herald*, April 2, 2017. https://www.miamiherald.com/news/nation-world/national/article142329269.html.

Hanh, T.N. 2017. "The Insight of Interbeing." Garrison Institute. https://www.garrisoninstitute.org/blog/insight-of-interbeing/.

Harvard T.H. Chan. 2020. "Black people more than three times as likely as white people to be killed during a police encounter." https://www.hsph.harvard.edu/news/hsph-in-the-news/blacks-whites-police-deaths-disparity/.

Hasset-Walker, C. 2019. "The racist roots of American policing: From slave patrols to traffic stops." *The Chicago Reporter*, June 7, 2019. https://www.chicagoreporter.com/the-racist-roots-of-american-policing-from-slave-patrols-to-traffic-stops/.

Hill, E. et al. 2021. "How George Floyd Was Killed in Police Custody." *The New York Times*, May 31, 2020. https://www.nytimes.com/2020/05/31/us/george-floyd-investigation.html.

Horowitz, S., M. Berman, and Wesley Lowery. 2017. "Sessions orders Justice Department to review all police reform agreements." *The Washington Post*, April 3, 2017. https://www.washingtonpost.com/world/national-security/sessions-orders-justice-department-to-review-all-police-reform-agreements/2017/04/03/ba934058-18bd-11e7-9887-1a5314b56a08_story.html.

Imarisha, W. 2016. "Oregon Black History Program in Portland." Walidah Imarisha. https://www.walidah.com/blog/2016/3/25/oregon-black-history-program-in-portland.

"Intrigue." 2021. Lexico.com. https://www.lexico.com/definition/intrigue.

Jacobo, J. 2016. "Experts on Why Police Aren't Trained to Shoot to Wound." ABC News, July 7, 2016. https://abcnews.go.com/US/police-trained-shoot-wound-experts/story?id=40402933.

Jones, L.D. 2004. "Sir Robert Peel's Nine Principles: Their Relevance to Campus Policing in the 21st Century." *Campus Law Enforcement Journal* (CLEJ) 34, no. 3. https://www.ojp.gov/ncjrs/virtual-library/abstracts/sir-robert-peels-nine-principles-their-relevance-campus-policing.

Kappa Alpha Psi Fraternity Inc. 2021. "A Brief History." https://kappaalphapsi1911.com/page/History.

Kaste, M. "NYPD Study: Implicit Bias Training Changes Minds, Not Necessarily Behavior." NPR, September 10, 2020. https://www.npr.org/2020/09/10/909380525/nypd-study-implicit-bias-training-changes-minds-not-necessarily-behavior.

Kelly, J. and M. Nichols. 2020. "We found 85,000 cops who've been investigated for misconduct. Now you can read their records." *USA Today News*, April 24, 2020. https://www.usatoday.com/in-depth/news/investigations/2019/04/24/usa-today-revealing-misconduct-records-police-cops/3223984002/.

Klein, C. 2020. "How Selma's 'Bloody Sunday' Became a Turning Point in the Civil Rights Movement." History. https://www.history.com/news/selma-bloody-sunday-attack-civil-rights-movement.

Lartey, J. 2017. "Former officer Michael Slager sentenced to 20 years for murder of Walter Scott." *The Guardian*, December 7, 2017. https://www.theguardian.com/us-news/2017/dec/07/michael-slager-walter-scott-second-degree-murder.

Law Enforcement Contacts Policy and Data Review Committee: 2016 Annual Report. 2017. https://03453d09-3cc0-403c-80f1-596fec523dcd.filesusr.com/ugd/e0b585_597a25d80eb04f2697fb825c3645e117.pdf.

Liang, S. and C. Wu. 1997. *Qigong Empowerment: A guide to Medical Taoist Buddhist Wushu Energy Cultivation.* The Way of the Dragon Publishing, East Providence, Rhode Island.

Lopez, G. 2017. "For years, this popular test measured anyone's racial bias. But it might not work after all." Vox, March 7, 2017. https://www.vox.com/identities/2017/3/7/14637626/implicit-association-test-racism.

MappingPoliceViolence.org. 2017. "2017 Police Violence Report." Accessed July 7, 2020. https://policeviolencereport.org/.

Mapping Police Violence. 2021. https://mappingpoliceviolence.org.

Massachusetts DCJIS. 2016. "Implementing CORI reform." https://www.mass.gov/files/documents/2016/09/sy/implementing-cori-reform.pdf.

Massachusetts.gov. 2021. "Speciality Courts." https://www.mass.gov/specialty-courts.

Maxfield, M. G., and E. Babbie. 2005. *Research Methods for Criminal Justice and Criminology*. Wadsworth Thomson Learning.

McCall, T. 2007. *Yoga as Medicine: The Yogic Prescription for Health and Healing*. New York: Bantam.

McCauley, M. and C. Casey. 2014. "The Comcast/Time Warner Cable Merger: A Bad Deal For Consumers." Consumer Reports, April 1, 2014. https://advocacy. consumerreports.org/research/the-comcast-time-warner-cable-merger-a-bad-deal-for-consumers/.

McGrath, M.A. 2019. "The 4 Best Examples of Police and Mental Health Response." Rave, November 21, 2019. https://www.ravemobilesafety.com/blog/best-examples-of-police-and-mental-health-response.

Mitchell, R.J. and L James. 2018. "Addressing the Elephant in the Room: The Need to Evaluate Implicit Bias Training Effectiveness for Improving Fairness in Police Officer Decision-Making." *Police Chief*. https://www.policechiefmagazine. org/addressing-the-elephant-in-the-room.

Morodenibig, N. L. 2011. *Philosophy Podium: A Dogon Perspective*. Firefly Productions, Chicago, Illinois.

Morodenibig, N. L. 1999. "The Great of Divine Ordinances, The Code of Human Behavior: Translation of the papyri Nw, Nbsni, and Insa." The Earth Center.

Murch, Donna. 2015. "Crack in Los Angeles: Crisis, Militarization, and Black Response to the Late Twentieth-Century War on Drugs." *Journal of American History* 102, no. 1. https://doi.org/10.1093/jahist/jav260.

Musgrave, S. 2019. "The Chemists and the Cover-Up." Reason, February 9, 2019. https://reason.com/2019/02/09/the-chemists-and-the-cover-up/.

Myers, B. 2020. "Sherman's Field Order No. 15." New Georgia Encyclopedia. https://www.georgiaencyclopedia.org/articles/history-archaeology/shermans-field-order-no-15.

National Archives. 1999. "Black Soldiers in the US Military During the Civil War." https://www.archives.gov/education/lessons/blacks-civil-war.

Nelson, L. and D. Lind. 2015. "The school to prison pipeline, explained." Justice Policy Institute. http://www.justicepolicy.org/news/8775.

News.Seattle.Gov. 2018. "Preliminary Findings of Fact, Conclusions of Law and Order Re: City Attorney's Motion to Dismiss Possession of Marijuana Charges." https://news.seattle.gov/wp-content/uploads/2018/09/MarijuanaOrder.pdf.

New York DoI. 2019. "Examination By Doi's Office Of The Inspector General For The Nypd Identifies Deficiencies And Recommends Improvements In How

NYPD Handles Complaints Of Biased Policing." https://www1.nyc.gov/assets/doi/reports/pdf/2019/Jun/19BiasRpt_62619.pdf.

Nokes, Greg. 2020. "Black Exclusion Laws in Oregon." Oregon Encyclopedia. https://www.oregonencyclopedia.org/articles/exclusion_laws/#.YFWOUC2ZOqA.

Oakland Wiki. 2017. "Miguel Masso." https://localwiki.org/oakland/Miguel_Masso.

Oppel, R.A., D.B. Taylor, and N. Bogel-Burroughs. 2021. "What to Know About Breonna Taylor's Death." *The New York Times*, January 6, 2021. https://www.nytimes.com/article/breonna-taylor-police.html.

Oregonian, The. 2017. "House Bill 2355." https://gov.oregonlive.com/bill/2017/HB2355/.

Office of Economic Analysis. 2010. Oregon's Demographic Trends.. www.oregon.gov/DAS/OEA/docs/demographic/OR_pop_trend2010.pdf?ga=t2010.

Oregon Legislative Information. 2019. "HB 3261 Enrolled." https://olis.leg.state.or.us/liz/2019r1/Measures/Overview/HB3216

Ortiz, E. 2015. "Freddie Gray: From Baltimore arrest to protests, a timeline of the case." MSNBC, May 1, 2015. https://www.msnbc.com/msnbc/freddie-gray-baltimore-arrest-protests-timeline-the-case-msna586321.

Pavelka, S. 2016. "Restorative Justice in the States: An Analysis of Statutory Legislation and Policy." *Justice Policy Journal* 2, no. 13. https://www.researchgate.net/publication/317007535_Restorative_Justice_in_the_States_An_Analysis_of_Statutory_Legislation_and_Policy.

PDX Flash Alert News. 2015. Community Conscious Policing Workshop Brings Law Enforcement and Community Leaders Together. pdx-fanews.blogspot.com/2015/05/community-conscious-policing-workshop.html/.

PHGL F. & A. M. of Massachusetts. "A Brief History of African Lodge." https://www.princehall.org/african-lodge-459/.

Pink, D. 2005. *A Whole New Mind: Why Right Brainers Will Rule the Future.* New York: Riverhead Books.

Prengaman, Peter. 2002. "Racist Statutes Under Siege." *Los Angeles Times,* September 29, 2002. http://articles.latimes.com/2002/sep/29/news/adna-racist299.

Queally, J. and Ben Poston. 2020. "California police agencies reject racial profiling complaints." *The Los Angeles Times,* December 14, 2020. https://www.latimes.com/california/story/2020-12-14/california-police-racial-profiling-complaints-rejected.

Rahman, A. 2007. *The Regime Change of Kwame Nkrumah: Epic Heroism in*

Africa and the Diaspora. London: Palgrave Macmillan.

Ratigan, E. 2010. "Cambridge officials unveil monument to Prince Hall." Wicked Local Cambridge, May 18, 2010. https://cambridge.wickedlocal.com/article/20100518/NEWS/305189834.

Raymond, K. 2013. "Black Freemasons have long history in Oklahoma." The Oklahoman, February 24, 2013. https://www.oklahoman.com/article/3757711/black-freemasons-have-long-history-in-oklahoma.

Rizzolatti, G. 2005. "The mirror neuron system and its function in humans." *Anatomy and Embryology* 210. https://doi.org/10.1007/s00429-005-0039-z.

Robert, H.M. 2020. *Robert's Rules of Order Newly Revised*. PublicAffairs.

Robinson, J. 2016. "For Black Men, Running Is a Reasonable Reaction to Police Harassment and Racial Profiling, Concludes Massachusetts' Supreme Court." ACLU. https://www.aclu.org/blog/criminal-law-reform/reforming-police/black-men-running-reasonable-reaction-police-harassment.

Schillinger, H. and E. Okuno. 2017. "COLOR BRAVE SPACE — HOW TO RUN A BETTER EQUITY FOCUSED MEETING." Fakequity, May 26, 2017. https://fakequity.com/2017/05/26/color-brave-space-how-to-run-a-better-equity-focused-meeting/.

Scott, L. "The history of Black sororities and fraternities." WCNC, February 4, 2021. https://www.wcnc.com/article/life/holidays/black-history-month/the-history-of-black-sororities-and-fraternities/275-4781f178-6f61-453e-94c7-2dd7ef06b1a3.

Shcager, N. 2020. "Netflix Takes You Inside the Massive Drug Scandal That Freed 35,000 People." The Daily Beast, April 1, 2020. https://www.thedailybeast.com/netflixs-how-to-fix-a-drug-scandal-takes-us-inside-the-massive-drug-scandal-that-freed-35000-people.

Smith, A. 1853. *The Theory of Moral Sentiments*. Henry G. Bohn.

State of Oregon. 2013. Oregon Education Investment Board: Equity Lens. www.ode.state.or.us/superintendent/priorities/final-equity-lens-draft-adopted.pdfi-f.

Stolberg, S.G. 2015. "Baltimore Enlists National Guard and a Curfew to Fight Riots and Looting." *The New York Times*, April 28, 2015. https://www.nytimes.com/2015/04/28/us/baltimore-freddie-gray.html.

Stole, B. 2017. "Former Marksville deputy marshal Derrick Stafford gets 40 years in boy's shooting death." *The Acadiana Advocate*, March 31, 2017. https://www.theadvocate.com/acadiana/news/courts/article_25dea6d0-1612-11e7-8e4c-1734ce7fb6e0.html.

Swaine, J. 2015. "Ferguson protests: state of emergency declared after violent night." *The Guardian*, August 10, 2015. https://www.theguardian.com/us-news/2015/aug/10/ferguson-protests-st-louis-state-of-emergency.

Taylor, D.B. 2021. "George Floyd Protests: A Timeline." *The New York Times*. March 28, 2021. https://www.nytimes.com/article/george-floyd-protests-timeline.html.

"Terror." Merriam-Webster. https://www.merriam-webster.com/dictionary/terror.

Thacher, D. 2001. "Equity and community policing: A new view of community partnerships." *Criminal Justice Ethics* 20, no.1. https://doi.org/10.1080/0731129X.2001.9992093.

Thich Nhat Hahn Foundation. 2017. "When Giants Meet," Thich Nhat Hahn Foundation.org, August 9, 2017. https://thichnhathanhfoundation.org/blog/2017/8/9/when-giants-meet.

"Transparency Data." 2021. Newark Police Department. http://npd.newark-publicsafety.org/statistics/transparency.

Trojanowicz, R. C., and B. Bucqueroux. 1994. *Community Policing: How to Get Started.* Anderson.

Tulsa Historical Society and Museum. 2021. "1921 Tulsa Race Massacre." https://www.tulsahistory.org/exhibit/1921-tulsa-race-massacre/.

Tuzzolo, E. and D.T. Hewitt. 2006. "Rebuilding Inequity: The Re-Emergence of the School-to-Prison Pipeline in New Orleans." *The High School Journal* 90, no. 2. https://doi.org/10.1353/hsj.2007.0009.

US Census Bureau (USCB). 2019. "Quick Facts." https://www.census.gov/quickfacts/fact/table/US/PST045219.

US Census Resident Population Data. http://2010.census.gov/2010census/data/apportionment-pop-text.php

US Department of Justice. 2018. "Department of Justice Coordinated Tribal Assistance Solicitation FY 18 Combined Award List – September 19, 2018." https://www.justice.gov/tribal/page/file/1095161/download.

U. S. Department of Justice. 2005. "What Is Community Policing?" www.cops.usdoj.gov/Default.asp?Item=2624.

Unidos, P. and J. Unidos. "Lessons in Racial Justice and Movement Building: Dismantling the School-to-Prison Pipeline in Colorado and Nationally." Advancement Project. https://b.3cdn.net/advancement/ad2cf09c7de156e4d2_b9m6i8ubh.pdf.

Walker, S.E. and C.A. Archbold. 2019. *The New World of Police Accountability*. Sage Publications.

Wesley, C. H. 2021. "Origin of Prince Hall Masonry." Most Worshipful Prince Hall Grand Lodge of Texas. https://www.mwphglotx.org/about-freemasonry/who-was-prince-hall/#

Wilson, V. 2016. "People of color will be a majority of the American working class in 2032: What this means for the effort to grow wages and reduce inequality." Economic Policy Institute. https://www.epi.org/publication/the-changing-demographics-of-americas-working-class/.

Zebley, K.R. 1998. "Rebel Salvation: The Story of Confederate Pardons. " University of Tennessee diss. https://trace.tennessee.edu/utk_graddiss/3629.

FURTHER REFERENCES

Compiled by Dr. G. Johnson, Cascade Academy

Agorist, M. 2017. "Cop Receives Unprecedented 40-Year Sentence for Killing 6yo Boy." The Free Thought Project. the-freethoughtproject.com/stafford-sentenced-jeremy-mardis-killing/.

Bernstein, M. 2016. "Police Chief Larry O'Dea Faced One More Investigation Before He Retired This Week." *The Oregonian*, June 2016. www.oregonlive.com/portland/index.ssf/2016/06/police_chief_larry_odea_faced.html

Bond, Graham, D. 2017. "Berkeley to Appoint New Police Chief, but Critics Say Department Lagging On Reforms." *East Bay Express*, April 4, 2017. m.eastbay-express.com/SevenDays/archives/2017/04/04/berkeley-to-appoint-new-police-chief-but-critics-say-department-lagging-on-reforms.

Bossip. 2017. "Cops Drop Case Against Deaf Black Man Accused of Resisting Orders He Couldn't Hear." bossip.com/1441687/cops-drop-case-against-deaf-black-man-accused-of-resisting-orders-he-couldnt-hear/.

Center, National Constitution. 1865. "13th Amendment: Abolition of Slavery." https://constitutioncenter.org/interactive-constitution/amendment/amendment-xiii.

Chappell, B. 2015. "For US children, Minorities Will Be the Majority by 2020, Census Says." Oregon Public Broadcasting, March 4, 2015. www.npr.org/sections/thetwo-way/2015/03/04/390672196/for-u-s-children-minorities-will-be-the-majority-by-2020-census-says.

Chretien, T. 2017. "Why Is This Cop Still In Uniform?" Socialist Worker, April 3, 2017. socialist-worker.org/2017/04/03/why-is-this-cop-still-in-uniform.

Creager, K. (2017). "City Government's Culture of Dismiss and Deny in the Face of Criticism: Editorial Agenda. 2017." The Oregonian, March 2017. www.oregonlive.com/opinion/index.ssf/2017/03/city_governments_culture_of_di.html#incart_river_-mobile_home.

Debolt, D. 2017. "Oakland Police Dept. Audit: Officer Recruitment, Misconduct Under Microscope." East Bay Times, February 1, 2017. www.eastbaytimes.com/2017/02/01/opd-audit-officer-recruitment-misconduct-under-microscope/.

Earth Center, The. "The Journey Leading Up to the EC." https://www.thee-arthcenter.org/history

East Bay Express. 2016. "New Lawsuit Alleges Oakland Police Conspiracy to Cover Up Home Invasion By Drunk Cops." m.eastbayexpress.com/SevenDays/archives/2016/10/28/new-lawsuit-alleges-oakland-police-conspiracy-to-cover-up-home-invasion-by-drunk-cops.

Elena, M. 2017. "Black Judge with History of Holding Cops Accountable Found Dead in River." The GED Section. thegedsection.com/blogs/black-judge-with-history-of-holding-cops-accountable-found-dead-in-river

Forman, Jr., J. 2017. "'Locking Up Our Own,'" What Led to Mass Incarceration of Black Men." The New York Times, April 11, 2017. mobile.nytimes.com/2017/04/11/books/review-locking-up-ourown-james-forman-jr.html.

Francis, N. 2017. "Rodney Hess Death Video: Man Streams Fatal Shooting by Police on Facebook Live." INQUISITR, May 3, 2017. www.inquisitr.com/4068843/rodney-hess-death-video-man-streams-fatal-shooting-by-police-on-facebook-live/.

Gettys, T. 2017. "Watch: Cops Tell Florida Woman to 'Stop Calling 911' 3 Hours before She Was Gunned Down by Boyfriend." Rawstory, April 2017. www.rawstory.com/2017/04/watch-cops-tell-florida-woman-to-stop-calling-911-3-hours-before-shewas-gunned-down-by-boyfriend/.

Gibson, L. S. 2020. "America's Oldest Civil Rights Organization – The Prince Hall Masons." Afro News. https://afro.com/americas-oldest-civil-rights-organization-the-prince-hall-masons/.

Good Morning America. 2017. "Colorado College Student Thrown to Ground by Police Says She Was 'Humiliated,' Calls for Police Change." ABC NEWS, April 13, 2017. gma.yahoo.com/colorado-college-student-thrown-ground-police-says-she-114805312--abc-news-topstories.html.

Grand Lodge D.C. 2021. Most Worshipful Prince Hall. "Famous Prince Hall Masons." http://www.mwphgldc.com/index.php/links/famous-ph-masons.

Green, A. 2017. "Video: Cop Who Yelled 'I'm Going to Shoot You in the Head!' Now Under Investigation." *The Oregonian*, April 2017. www.oregon-live.com/portland/index.ssf/2017/04/video -cop who yelled im going.html#incart river home.

Guardian, The. 2015. "The Counted: People killed by police in the US." https://www.theguardian.com/us-news/ng-interactive/2015/jun/01/the-counted-police-killings-us-database.

Harriot, M. 2017. "According to Republicans, Black People Are Stupid and Lazy." The Root, April 3, 2017. www.theroot.com/according-to-republicans-black-people-are-stupid-and-l-1793967234.

Harriot, M. 2017. "Yes, You Can Measure White Privilege." The Root April 14, 2017. https://www.theroot.com/yes-you-can-measure-white-privilege-1794303451.

Hauser, C. 2017. "Wyclef Jean Is Briefly Detained and Handcuffed in Los Angeles." *The New York Times*, March 21, 2017. mobile.nytimes.com/2017/03/21/arts/music/wyclef-jean-handcuffed.html.

Hilliard, J. 2017. "Brookline Seeks To Fire Two Officers Who Complained of Racial Discrimination." *The Boston Globe*, March 3, 2017 . https://www.bostonglobe.com/metro/2017/03/03/brookline-seeks-fire-two-officers-who-complained-racial-discrimination/TPUKmV4gEvyJMZMS48NpJL/story.html

Horwitz, S., M. Berman, and W. Lowery. 2017. "Sessions Orders Justice Dept. Review of All Police Reform Agreements, Including Ferguson." *St. Louis Post Dispatch*, April 3, 2017. www.stltoday.com/news/national/sessions-orders-justice-dept-review-of-all-police-reform-agreements/article d7a366f1-25ef-5983-9729-c095f8d56aac.html.

Jarrett, L. 2017. "Federal Judge in Baltimore Approves Sweeping Plan for Police." CNN, April 7, 2017. www.cnn.com/2017/04/07/politics/baltimore-police-justice-department-reforms/index.html?sr=twCNN040717baltimore-police-justice-department-reforms0445PMStoryLink&linkId=36300216.

Jones, C. 2017. How America Kills Black Men without Lifting a Finger." Huffington Post, March 10, 2017. www.huffingtonpost.com/entry/is-stress-killing-black-men_us_58c2b6f8e4b0c3276fb783c8.

Kindelan, K. 2017. "Police Officer Turns Call About Alleged Fight into Dance Off with College Students." Good Morning America. www.yahoo.com/gma/police-officer-turns-call-alleged-fight-dance-off-192405965--abc-news-topstories.html.

Knapp, A. 2017. "Charleston Jury Awards $1.3M to Black Couple Who Accused Trooper of Racial Profiling." The Post and Courier. www.postandcourier.com/news/charleston-jury-awards-m-to-black-couple-who-accused-trooper/article_d583b24a-09df-11e7-a743-6f08f0b3fa6c.html.

Lay, J., B. Western, K. C. M. von Baldegg, and T. N. Coates. 2015. "Mass Incarceration, Visualized." The Atlantic, September 1, 2015. www.theatlantic.com/video/index/404890/prison-inherited-trait/.

Leonnig, C. D. 2017. "Secret Service Agrees to Pay $24 Million in Decades Old Race Bias Case Brought by Black Agents." The Washington Post, January 17, 2017. www.washingtonpost.com/politics/secret-service-agrees-to-pay-24-million-to-settle-decades-old-race-bias-case-brought-by-black-agents/2017/01/17/b386006e-dd23-11e6-ad42-f3375f-271c9c_story.html?utm_term=.b5663acac5f7.

Lever, R. 2017. "US Resistance Movement Coalesces…on Twitter." AFP. www.msn.com/en-us/news/politics/us-resistance-movement-coalesces-on-twitter/ar-AAmkSmj?li=BBnb7Kz.

Library of Congress. 2017. "Prince Hall Freemasonry: A Resource Guide." https://guides.loc.gov/prince-hall-freemasonry/videos.

Lohr, D. 2017. "Cop Filmed Beating Unarmed Man, Pulling Gun and Ordering Crowd 'the Fu**K Back'." Huffington Post, March 13, 2017. www.huffingtonpost.com/entry/vallejo-police-beating-video_us_58c6a7d8e4b0ed71826dfcfa?%3Futm_hp_ref=black-voices&ir=Black%2BVoices.

Maxwell, F. 2017. "This Is Why We Must Continue To Say 'Black Lives Matter.'" The Huffington Post, April 15, 2017. www.huffingtonpost.com/entry/two-curb-stomps-in-the-same-week-this-is-whywe-say_us_58efe790e4b0156697224daa?ncid=engmodushpmg00000003.

McCluskey, M. 2017. "This Former Philadelphia Cop Had An Incredibly Simple Plan to Keep Kids Out of Prison. Don't Arrest Them." The Washington Post, March 30, 2017. www.washingtonpost.com/news/inspired-life/wp/2017/03/30/this-former-philadelphia-cop-had-an-incredibly-simple-plan-to-keep-kids-out-of-prison-dont-arrest-them/?ut-m_term=.de19f2427aab.

McGirt, E. 2016. "Why Race and Culture Matter in the C-Suite." *Fortune.* fortune.com/black-executives-men-c-suite/?xid=for_fb_sh.

Mosely, K. 2018. "10 Ways to Practice Institutional Racism at Your Non-Profit Organization." https://korbettmosesly.com/blog/f/10-ways-to-practice-institutional-racism-at-your-non-profit/.

Moser, W. 2017. "Chicago Isn't Just Segregated, It Basically Invented Modern Segregation." *Chicago*, March 31, 2017. https://www.chicagomag.com/city-life/March-2017/Why-Is-Chicago-So-Segregated/.

New York Post. 2017. "Lying Cop Doesn't Know Uber Driver Is Actually a Lawyer." nypost.com/video/lying-cop-doesnt-known-uber-driver-was-actually-a-lawyer/.

Phillips, K. 2017. "Thousands of ICE Detainees Forced into Labor, a Violation of Anti-Slavery Laws." *The Washington Post.* www.msn.com/en-us/news/us/thousands-of-ice-detain-ees-claim-they-were-forced-into-labor-a-violation-of-anti-slavery-laws/ar-AAnOvss?li=BBnb7Kz.

Rhea, D. 2017. "Texas School Triples Recess Time, Solves Attention Deficit Disorder." Live The Organic Dream. livetheorganicdream.com/texas-school-triples-recess-time-solves-attention-deficit-disorder/.

Roecker, M. 2017. "Video Show Cop Slam, Beat Black Man After Alleged Jaywalking." NBC News. www.msn.com/en-us/news/us/video-shows-cop-slam-beat-black-man-after-alleged-jaywalking/ar-BBzJYnx?ocid=twmsn.

Ryan, L. 2017. "Ten Unmistakable Signs of a Fear-Based Workplace." *Forbes,* March 7, 2017. www.forbes.com/sites/lizryan/2017/03/07/ten-unmistakable-signs-of-a-fear-based-workplace/#630e03801e26.

Schuppe, J. 2017. "Wrongfully Convicted Man Get 175,000 for 13 Years in Prison." NBC News Online. www.msn.com/en-us/news/us/wrongfully-convicted-man-gets-dollar175000-for-13-years-in-prison/ar-AAo39mU?li=BBnb7Kz.

Smith, M. (2017). "New Ferguson Video Adds Wrinkle to Michael Brown Case." *The New York Times*, March 11, 2017. mobile.nytimes.com/2017/03/11/us/michael-brown-ferguson-police-shooting-video.html?_r=0&referer=.

Van Der Woo, L. 2017. "Black Riders Face Stiffest Transit Penalty at Rates More Than Six Times That of Whites." Investigate West, April 5, 2017. invw.org/2017/04/05/black-riders-face-stiffest-transit-penalty/.

Velasquez-Manoff, M. 2017. "What Biracial People Know." *The New York Times*, March 4, 2017. mobile.nytimes.com/2017/03/04/opinion/sunday/what-biracial-people-know.html?_r=1&referer=.

Willis, J. 2017. "Kendall Jenner 'Devastated' Over Pulled Pepsi Ad Controversy—Is This a Career Breaker?" ET Online. www.msn.com/en-us/tv/celebrity/exclusive-kendall-jenner-devastated-over-pulled-pepsi-ad-controversy-is-this-a-career-breaker/ar-BBzs2j7?li=BBnb7Kz.

Winston, A. and D.B. Graham. 2016. "Badge of Dishonor: Top Oakland Police Department Officials Looked Away as East Bay Cops Sexually Exploited and Trafficked a Teenager." *East Bay Express,* June 15, 2016. https://eastbayexpress.com/badge-of-dishonor-top-oakland-police-department-officials-looked-away-as-east-bay-cops-sexually-exploited-and-trafficked-a-teenager-2-1/

Wootson, C.R. 2017. "A California Waiter Refused to Serve 4 Latina Customers until He Saw 'Proof Of Residency.'" *The Washington Post,* March 18, 2017. www.washingtonpost.com/news/post-nation/wp/2017/03/19/a-california-waiter-refused-to-serve-4-latina-women-until-he-saw-proof-of-residency/?utm_term=.55f6f010fe73/

Wootson, C.R. 2017. "Body Cam Captures Cop's Violent Encounter with Teen." *The Washington Post,* April 6, 2017. www.washingtonpost.com/news/post-nation/wp/2017/04/06/a-body-cam-captured-a-cops-violent-encounter-with-a-teen-but-a-new-law-keeps-the-video-secret/?utm_term=.c2c022ad4f8e.

Wootson, C.R. 2017. "A Handcuffed 14-Year-Old Girl Spat at an Officer. He Punched Her Face—and Claimed Self-Defense." The Washington Post, . www.msn.com/en-us/news/us/a-handcuffed-14-year-old-girl-spat-at-an-officer-he-punched-her-face-%E2%80%94-and-claimed-self-defense/ar-AAmeG3W?li=BBnb7Kz.

Young, D. 2017. "The 10 Most Dangerous Types of Supposedly 'Cool' White People." The Root, March 14, 2017. https://verysmartbrothas.theroot.com/the-10-most-dangerous-types-of-supposedly-cool-white-1822521370

Acknowledgments

Thank you to the Department of Public Safety Standards and Training in Salem, Oregon; FBI National Academy Associates, Oregon chapter; and to the City of Corvallis Police Department and Mayor of Corvallis, Julie Manning, for supporting the Community Conscious Policing workshops centered on Best Practices in Community Conscious Policing.

Training 4 Transformation, LLC, would especially like to acknowledge and thank the hundreds of community members and organizations that volunteered their time, traveled, and participated. None of this would have been possible without the talented Training 4 Transformation, LLC, facilitation team, staff, and volunteers who are bilingual, trained in experiential learning, and have lived or worked internationally, all while maintaining local roots in their respective communities.

The collective efforts of the law enforcement agencies, community organizations, and cities who contributed to an unprecedented statewide event are truly appreciated!

About the Author

COMMUNITY CONSCIOUS POLICING ®©

Community Conscious Policing is a curriculum that we designed and implemented to train law enforcement worldwide. It consists of a Culturally Proficient, Equitable, and Empathetic approach to community engagement based on T4T's 21st century Conscious Leadership principles.

MEET BRANDON LEE

Cofounder of Training 4 Transformation (T4T), Brandon is a proud Black man from Oakland, California, and Houston, Texas. With a lifetime of experience personally advocating for justice against profiling and institutional racism, he has become the expert in transforming traumatic circumstances into hopeful, victorious ones. His understanding of how to correct and restore institutions to a healthy and inclusive environment is unmatched. Brandon is a regular presenter and speaker at educational institutions, government agencies, nonprofit organizations, and conferences on topics that include:

How to Survive a Police Stop

Community Solutions to Policing

Racism, Trauma & Healing

Black Founders of the United States of America

Community Conscious Policing

BOOK

As a survivor of racial profiling, Mr. Lee was awarded a monetary settlement that resulted in disciplinary actions against the officers involved. In Oakland, he worked to fund the Citizens Police Review Board, which was later replaced by the Police Commission and Community Police Review Agency in 2016 (Measure LL). Recently, T4T was hired by the Mayor's Office to establish the Portland Committee on Community Engaged Policing. It satisfied the final requirements of the settlement agreement between the United States Department of Justice and City of Portland.

EDUCATION

Brandon was the only Black male in his class admitted to the prestigious College Preparatory High School in Oakland (Ranked #1 Best Private High School in California, and #4 nationally by Niche). He went on to double major in Spanish and public policy at Houston Baptist University. Brandon is regarded as an Internationalist by the School for International Training where he earned a Master of Arts degree in Teaching (MAT) English to Speakers of Other Languages.

Internationally, he has studied Spanish language and culture in Spain and international business at the University of Havana, Cuba (UH). He also taught English as a Foreign Language at the University of Mexico (UAEH). The highlight of his travels was hearing Nelson Mandela, the first Black President of South Africa, speak at the International AIDs Conference in Barcelona.

ABOUT THE AUTHOR

EXPERIENCE

At the University of San Diego, Mr. Lee served as a Teacher Trainer/ Language and Culture Coach where he taught a live 150-hour certification class in Teaching English to Speakers of Other Languages (TESOL). He is well known for bringing a globally minded lens to local situations. After teaching as a faculty member in higher education, Brandon stepped into leadership as the Retention & Multicultural Center Coordinator at Portland Community College and Director of the Center for Fraternity and Sorority Life at Oregon State University.

Brandon enjoyed a successful career teaching Harvard Business Case Studies to international students and professionals earning a Masters in Business Administration (MBA) from the University of Delaware and Oregon State University.

At PCC, Mr. Lee co-chaired the diversity council with the campus president. Collectively, they served "to address the problems of racism, sexism, classism, heterosexism, and other forms of oppression within the campus community." Under his leadership at OSU, the Center for Fraternity and Sorority Life worked in collaboration to bring the first Native American sorority, first Latin-based fraternity, first historically Black sorority, and a student chapter of the NAACP on campus. These diverse organizations served as mechanisms of retention for some of the most vulnerable students and their presence was unprecedented at Oregon State University, a predominantly White institution. As faculty adviser, Mr. Lee supported the African Student Association, historically Black Greek letter organizations, and Multicultural Unified Greek Council on campus.

CIVIC ENGAGEMENT

Civically, Brandon was appointed to the governor-appointed Oregon Law Enforcement Data Collection and Policy Review Committee (LECC).

As a board member, Brandon worked to pass HB2355, which required law enforcement agencies to collect and submit data on the age, race, ethnicity and sex of a person contacted during a traffic or pedestrian stop.

The bill mandated that the Oregon Criminal Justice Commission and, later, the Department of Public Safety Standards and Training review the data by July 2020 and provide assistance to agencies struggling with profiling.

The measure also charged people caught with user-level amounts of cocaine, methamphetamine and heroin with misdemeanors instead of felonies, replacing jail time with mandatory treatment. It reduced the charge so non-residents in the United States legally on a visa, green card or with refugee status would not be automatically deported based on a user-level drug conviction.

Oregon became the first state in the United States to decriminalize the possession of all drugs on Nov. 3, 2020. Measure 110 passed with more than 58% of the vote Dec 10, 2020 (USA News By Scott Akins and Clayton Mosher).

COMMUNITY AFFILIATIONS

For community service, Brandon volunteered to help transform the NAACP Corvallis/Albany Branch as their Legal Redress Committee Chairman and served as the first Grand Historian for M.W. Prince Hall Grand Lodge of Oregon, Idaho & Montana Jurisdiction, Inc. Additionally, Mr. Lee led the Police Accountability Team as a congregant of the First Unitarian Church of Portland and is a proud member of the Scottish Rite of Freemasonry (S.J.), Prince Hall Shriners, Kappa Alpha Psi Fraternity, Inc., and a global initiate of the M'TAM School of Kem Philosophy and Spirituality at The Earth Center.